PROVERBS FOR YOU

KATHLEEN NIELSON
PROVERBS FOR YOU

thegoodbook
COMPANY

Proverbs For You

© Kathleen Nielson, 2020. Reprinted 2022.

Published by:
The Good Book Company

thegoodbook.com | www.thegoodbook.co.uk
thegoodbook.com.au | thegoodbook.co.nz | thegoodbook.co.in

ISBN: 9781784984274

Cover design by Ben Woodcraft | Printed in India

CONTENTS

SERIES PREFACE

Each volume of the *God's Word For You* series takes you to the heart of a book of the Bible, and applies its truths to your heart.

The central aim of each title is to be:

- Bible centred
- Christ glorifying
- Relevantly applied
- Easily readable

You can use *Proverbs For You:*

To read. You can simply read from cover to cover, as a book that explains and explores the themes, encouragements and challenges of this part of Scripture.

To feed. You can work through this book as part of your own personal regular devotions, or use it alongside a sermon or Bible-study series at your church. Each chapter is divided into two (or occasionally three) shorter sections, with questions for reflection at the end of each.

To lead. You can use this as a resource to help you teach God's word to others, both in small-group and whole-church settings. You'll find tricky verses or concepts explained using ordinary language, and helpful themes and illustrations along with suggested applications.

These books are not commentaries. They assume no understanding of the original Bible languages, nor a high level of biblical knowledge. Verse references are marked in **bold** so that you can refer to them easily. Any words that are used rarely or differently in everyday language outside the church are marked in gray when they first appear, and are explained in a glossary towards the back. There, you'll also find details of resources you can use alongside this one, in both personal and church life.

Our prayer is that as you read, you'll be struck not by the contents of this book, but by the book it's helping you open up; and that you'll praise not the author of this book, but the One he is pointing you to.

Carl Laferton, Series Editor

Bible translations used:

- ESV: English Standard Version (this is the version being quoted unless otherwise stated)

- NIV: New International Version, 2011 edition

- KJV: King James Version (also known as the Authorized Version)

INTRODUCTION TO PROVERBS

Wanted: Wisdom

Human beings are and always have been in need of wisdom. Wisdom helps us make decisions about what work to do; what to say (or not say); what person to marry (or avoid). Wisdom points us to habits that tend to make life smoother and happier. Wisdom gives shape and meaning to our cries of both suffering and delight. In general, wisdom offers insight into the concrete experiences of human life.

That's the commonly understood sense of wisdom. Who is not in need of it? Cultures throughout history have given ear to various sorts of **sages** who passed on their wisdom through words; today, we have popular bloggers, personal life coaches, authors of best-sellers about success, health, and happiness. Many people look for wisdom to well-known media figures like the American Oprah Winfrey, whose self-empowering sayings have been collected and recorded on dozens of website pages—Oprah's proverbs, you might say!

The Bible offers **God-breathed*** wisdom. This wisdom is utterly recognizable in that (like popular wisdom) it offers insight into the concrete experiences of human life. But it's also utterly different. The Bible's wisdom offers godly insight into the concrete experiences of human life in a world created and ruled by the Lord God of the Scriptures.

Although wisdom writing appears throughout the Scriptures, three "wisdom books" stand out: Job, Proverbs, and Ecclesiastes (with Song of Solomon often included). These books offer God-breathed wisdom in varying tones—like different kinds of music. Job and Ecclesiastes are like somber symphonies, engaging life's deepest, darkest questions. Song of Solomon is more like a lyrical opera, celebrating the love of husband and wife. Proverbs is more like a piano lesson, covering scales and basic chords—the stuff that makes up all the music—although

---

* Words in **gray** are defined in the Glossary (page 243).

it regularly breaks out into songs of various styles. The wisdom book of Proverbs addresses the spectrum of human activities and concerns that make up daily life: from eating and drinking, to the way we speak to one another, to family and social relationships, to sex, to business dealings, and on and on.

The more we read the book of Proverbs, the more we understand our need for its wisdom to speak into our often chaotic daily experiences. The wisdom of Proverbs calls us to see all the experiences of our lives in relation to the Lord who created and rules the world, who calls us first to fear him, and who himself shows us how.

Alert: Mind the Shape!

Proverbs acknowledges and even reflects the random-feeling progression of activities and concerns that fill our days. At the same time, this book comes to us carefully shaped by writers and editors led by God as they assembled and arranged this part of his holy Scriptures. The basic outline of Proverbs is clear:

1. Prologue (1:1-7)

2. The Foundation of Wisdom (1:8 – 9:18)

3. The Proverbs of Solomon (10:1 – 22:16)

4. The Words of the Wise (22:17 – 24:22)

5. More Sayings of the Wise (24:23-34)

6. The Proverbs of Solomon copied by King Hezekiah's Men (25:1 – 29:27)

7. The Words of Agur (30:1-33)

8. The Words of King Lemuel (31:1-9)

9. Epilogue (31:10-31)

I read Proverbs for too many years without paying close attention to the way this piece of wisdom literature holds together from beginning to end. Now, there is benefit in isolating and learning from Proverbs' distinct themes; many, myself included, have organized studies around the book's teachings on topics like words, work, family, friendships, generosity, the heart, and of course first and foremost the **fear of the Lord**.

But we must be on the alert when we rearrange this book into an order that satisfies us. The greatest risk is that we might not fully receive the book as it is given to us, in God's **sovereign** plan, from beginning to end. For the sake of clarity and efficiency, we might miss not the brilliance of the individual themes but rather the crucial relationship of the parts. We might overlook the way individual proverbs echo and play back and forth within and among passages. We might not see how the big chunks of the book together inform our most basic understanding of how to seek and process godly wisdom.

A predominantly thematic focus also could distract from careful attention to the shape of the poetry—originally written in Hebrew but amazingly accessible to us in translation. Part of what we must notice (and delight in) is the way the poetic form is wedded to the thematic and **theological** content. For example, part of what helps us to understand wisdom's two paths of wisdom and folly is the pairing of poetic lines, many of which express the contrast of these two ways. Not until we get to Proverbs 10 will we stop and discuss the poetry in detail, but at every point we will be noticing how the poetry works: through **parallelism** and vivid imagery that, in artfully condensed form, call us to wisdom.

A reasonably short treatment of Proverbs like this one can only begin to take account of the whole book, with its wealth of insights. But let's begin. Let's see how the first nine chapters establish a foundation for all that follows—a foundation that keeps reappearing and even deepening, at crucial points in the book. Let's taste the flavors of the various proverb collections built on that foundation, and let's hear the themes develop and wind around one another—kind of like they do in a day of real life!

I hope this trip through Proverbs will help make the book shine, as a beautifully shaped call to hear and follow wisdom from our Lord. I hope this will be an overview that inspires lifelong deep digging into the wisdom of Proverbs. We need this wisdom. And this wisdom comes to us in a remarkable book of wisdom literature, which we do well first to read and study in its God-given literary form.

Ahead: Jesus Shining

The book of Proverbs has sometimes been held in low regard for seemingly lacking the gospel-rich content that we find, for example, in the **Pentateuch**, which tells us redemption's story, or in the prophetic writings that point to a servant-king. Proverbs doesn't talk much about where and how to worship. It almost seems kind of... worldly.

Proverbs is worldly indeed, in that it shows godly wisdom infusing every part of God's created world. That's the point. Nothing in this world has meaning apart from the Creator of all things. Everything has meaning in relation to the One who in the beginning created the heavens and the earth and everything in them.

> Proverbs is worldly, in that it shows godly wisdom infusing every part of God's world. That's the point.

We will see that Proverbs does not establish as its foundation an abstract truth about God, the sovereign Creator and Ruler. No, Proverbs sets forth a foundational relationship with this Lord God: one that involves fearing him. Here is the decisive distinction between commonly understood wisdom and the Bible's wisdom: the Bible's wisdom calls us into a relationship with the Lord—a relationship that transforms every part of our lives, forever.

The Scriptures unfold the salvation that makes possible a relationship between **fallen**, sinful people and their holy Creator. God so loved the world that he gave his only Son (John 3:16). That Son became flesh and dwelt in the world he created; Jesus lived out the worldly wisdom that Proverbs is all about. In fact, Jesus is the worldly wisdom that Proverbs is all about. The New Testament affirms Christ as our "wisdom from God" (1 Corinthians 1:24). In him "are hidden all the treasures of wisdom and knowledge" (Colossians 2:3). This is the Christ who bore our sin and died suffering God's wrath in our place, and who rose from the dead, our resurrected Savior.

The treasures of wisdom hidden in Christ are eternal treasures: Jesus Christ is the eternal second Person of the **Godhead**. There has never been wisdom anywhere else but in him, from eternity past. The various poetic pictures of wisdom in Proverbs point us nowhere but to the source.

But let's dig in. Much better than talking about Proverbs' pictures is looking at them. Much better than asserting the book's shape is finding it in the text. And much better than theorizing about wisdom is listening to wisdom as God speaks in his **inspired** word. Looking and listening, we will indeed hear God's voice and see his Son shining through the book of Proverbs.

1. MEETING WISDOM

This first chapter introduces us to Proverbs' wisdom. Part One sets this wisdom in its layers of context and begins to dig into the book's prologue (Proverbs **1:1-7***). Part Two further explores the prologue, summing up what we can learn about this wisdom from the start. Proverbs' winding opening lines draw us in to the treasures—and the riddles—of this book.

Wisdom: The Larger Context

It is good to know that all human beings need wisdom. Not one of us is alone in reaching out for insight into common experiences such as getting along with our neighbors, or handling our money, or deciding whether and whom to marry. Chatting with a friend this morning, I needed wisdom on whether or not to reopen a subject of conversation—one that in my opinion had not reached good resolution between us. I'm still not sure whether I should have raised the matter again, which I did! But I *am* sure that I am not the only one who struggles to measure my words rightly.

The need for wisdom is a universal one. I'm writing these words in Jakarta, Indonesia. Just this afternoon, while waiting for a coffee at a local bookstore/coffee shop, I perused the nearest bookshelf of paperbacks offered in English. The first one that caught my eye was by a Japanese writer offering the secret to a long and happy life. There was a book on the Danish way to live well, and one by a French author on how to live better and longer. A little American gift book was all about happiness and how to achieve it. Here was a whole world of aspiring

---

* All Proverbs verse references being looked at in each chapter part are in **bold**.

wisdom writers, in a little Indonesian coffee shop! How desperately we humans reach out for wisdom, all over the globe.

Centuries ago, God's people living in the kingdom of Israel also knew this universal need for wisdom. They knew it partly because many nations around them in the ancient world had a special class of wisdom speakers and writers, often serving as advisors to kings. The Bible itself gives us clues: the book of Esther, for example, tells of the Persian king's "wise men who knew the times" (Esther 1:13)— although those wise men were anything but wise. The wisdom of Solomon that we find in Proverbs was known not only in Israel: "Solomon's wisdom surpassed the wisdom of all the people of the east and all the wisdom of Egypt ... and people of all nations came to hear the wisdom of Solomon, and from all the kings of the earth, who had heard of his wisdom" (1 Kings 4:30, 34).

Egypt in particular was renowned for its wisdom literature, of which a good number of ancient texts remain in evidence. Many **commentators** note the similarities of some of these texts to various aspects of the book of Proverbs. The Egyptians also used the form of father-son instructions that we see in Proverbs. Even more specific parallels can be found between sections of Proverbs 22 – 24 and the Egyptian *Instructions of Amenemope* (see Wilson, *Proverbs: An Introduction and Commentary*, page 4). As it turned out, my experience in the Indonesian shop was not a new thing! From all directions in Old Testament times—Egypt, Arabia, Babylon, Phoenicia—came voices offering insight into the concrete experiences of human life.

Solomon's Wisdom: Alike and Different

Why did Solomon's wisdom stand out? Many of the surrounding nations might not have known how to answer that question. In general, the people in those nations did not acknowledge the Lord God of the Scriptures, the One Creator God by whose **common grace** they were able to gain some insight into how his world works and how we can best live in it. Solomon was blessed to be part of the people who directly received God's revelation of himself—and through whom that revelation was offered to the world, ultimately through the Lord Jesus. We should note that the content of Proverbs was not all written by Solomon; certain sections of the book are attributed to other wise men. But the great majority of the sayings are indeed attributed to him, and the book's introduction points to him directly, as we will see.

Scripture itself highlights and explains Solomon's distinctive wisdom: "God gave Solomon wisdom and understanding beyond measure, and breadth of mind like the sand on the seashore" (1 Kings 4:29). God had spoken to King Solomon in a dream and invited him to make a request of God. Solomon humbly asked for wisdom—for "an understanding mind to govern your people, that I may discern between good and evil" (1 Kings 3:9). His request was granted: "Behold, I give you a wise and discerning mind, so that none like you has been before you and none like you shall arise after you" (1 Kings 3:12). Solomon's wisdom, then, was insight like that of the peoples around, but it was different: it was *God-given* insight into how to live in God's world.

We understand the distinctiveness of Proverbs today in how we receive it: as part of a whole God-breathed revelation given to us in the Scriptures of the Old and New Testaments. The Bible's wisdom books give inspired insight into the concrete experiences of human life in a world created and ruled by the Lord God of the Scriptures. It is a world created perfectly but which then fell, through human rebellion against the Creator. What mercy, that the Creator did not turn away and leave his creation in darkness without him. What grace, that the Creator had an eternal plan of redemption, through the Lord Jesus Christ who would come into this world and through whom God would **redeem** a people for himself from all the nations.

In Proverbs we break into the story of redemption revealed by God in his word. The biblical context is clear in the prologue, which introduces us to the wisdom offered in this book. The very first verse tells us the very first thing we need to know.

Proverbs' Clear Context

Sometimes called the "title," Proverbs **1:1** introduces not just the prologue but the book: "The proverbs of Solomon, son of **David**, king
of Israel." Those words tell us the first important thing to know: *Proverbs' wisdom comes in the context of God's word and God's people.*
Those three proper names (Solomon, David, and Israel) in one quick
sweep light up the entire Old Testament history of God calling out a
people for himself. Solomon was not just a wise king who wrote many
of these proverbs; he came from somewhere—in fact from the line of
David, of the tribe of Judah: one tribe of the Israelite people who grew
from Abraham into a great nation according to the Lord's promises.
These names make the history spring to life, and they set the book of
Proverbs in the most important context: that of all the Old Testament
books surrounding it.

In many ways it can be challenging to fit the wisdom books into
the pattern of Old Testament Scriptures. We often speak of the Bible's overarching narrative, its big story—the story of God's redeeming a people, through his Son. And we understand the different
kinds of books in relation to that story. The historical books unfold
the story largely in narrative. The prophetic books let us hear God's
voice speaking into the story through his called-out prophets. The
poetry of the Psalms gives us voices of people living the story and
crying out to God from inside it. So—how does the wisdom literature relate to the story?

The commentator Derek Kidner says that the wisdom books are
the point in the Old Testament "when the pilgrim is free to stop
and take a long look round, observing and asking questions about
all he sees" (*The Wisdom of Proverbs, Job, and Ecclesiastes*, page
11). In other words, the wisdom writers act like commentators on
the story. They've not written to advance the story, to speak like
prophets into the story, or to cry out from the midst of the story;
instead, they've stepped aside for a few moments to make observations about the story.

Even though this position of commentator somewhat separates the wisdom writers from the Bible's ongoing story, everything they say relates to that story. This "wisdom" was not a new or foreign concept for the Israelites; in fact, wisdom had always been connected to God and to his revealed word. In Deuteronomy 4:6, for example, as **Moses** is commanding obedience to the law given to them by God, he tells the people:

> "Keep [his commands] and do them, for that will be your wisdom and your understanding in the sight of the peoples, who, when they hear all these statutes, will say, 'Surely this great nation is a wise and understanding people.'"

Moses clearly knew it: wisdom comes in the context of God's word and God's people. God's revelation to his people is the "ground zero" of biblical wisdom. No nation today is built on that ground; only God's people, now the church, have such a foundation. That foundation is ultimately Christ himself, our wisdom from God fully revealed, perfectly lived out. The wisdom books help lay that foundation; they follow the trajectory of Old Testament teaching, which makes godly wisdom and God's revealed word utterly inseparable for God's people.

God's word has always reached into every aspect of human life. If you've made your way through Exodus and Leviticus, you've probably wondered at all those laws that address not just rituals of worship but also subjects like birds' nests, and detailed food regulations, and the construction of balconies on roofs, and clothing fabrics, and on and on. To those in Israel who knew God's revealed law and its comprehensive wisdom, a book like Proverbs might have seemed not set apart but utterly integral to the story of salvation that they were living out day by day.

All this means that we will read Proverbs securely in the context of the Scriptures, as part of the revelation of God's **redemptive work** carried out through the nation of Israel and climaxing in the One who brought blessing to all the nations through his death and resurrection—the Lord Jesus Christ. We won't skip these wisdom books but will indeed pore over them and celebrate the light they shed on the whole story.

If we were reading the autobiography of a wealthy landowner and estate-builder, we might be tempted to skip his chapters describing the details of his estate and how it runs. Those chapters might not seem crucial to the story. On the other hand, those details might light up the landowner for us, letting us see just who he is and how he works. And if we somehow find ourselves living on his estate, those details could be invaluable…

Kaleidoscopic Wisdom

As we make our way into Proverbs' opening verses, we see more specifically how this book leads us to think about the wisdom it offers. Looking at Proverbs **1:1**, we've already made the first of five observations: Proverbs' wisdom comes in the context of God's word and God's people. The five observations will unfold in this order, throughout the rest of this chapter:

1. Proverbs' wisdom comes in the context of God's word and God's people.

2. Proverbs' wisdom has kaleidoscopic meaning.

3. Proverbs' wisdom is found in relationship with the Lord.

4. Proverbs' wisdom is the alternative to folly.

5. Proverbs' wisdom stretches through God's revelation, revealed fully in Christ.

Let's get ready for the second observation by reading the prologue in its entirety:

"The proverbs of Solomon, son of David, king of Israel:
To know wisdom and instruction,
    to understand words of insight,
to receive instruction in wise dealing,
    in righteousness, justice, and equity;

to give prudence to the simple,
    knowledge and discretion to the youth—
Let the wise hear and increase in learning,
    and the one who understands obtain guidance,
to understand a proverb and a saying,
    the words of the wise and their riddles.
The fear of the LORD is the beginning of knowledge;
    Fools despise wisdom and instruction." (**v 1-7**)

The second observation is this: *Proverbs' wisdom has kaleidoscopic meaning.* Many people have tried to organize and categorize all the words relating to wisdom in Proverbs' prologue. The process can be frustrating! I call them "weighty wisdom words"—and we have quite an assorted package here. "Wisdom" comes first (**v 2**) and echoes throughout (**v 3, 5, 6, 7**). But this wisdom connects to a pattern of intertwined and interrelated vocabulary: "wisdom," "instruction," "understanding," "insight," "wise deal-ing," "righteousness," "justice," "eq-uity," "prudence," "knowledge," "dis-cretion," "learning," "guidance." Each word suggests a slightly different angle on the process of learning this wisdom. Together, the words suggest the com-plexity of the process.

> This book resists neat packaging. We should acknowledge that and even enjoy it.

If we're looking for what we might think we'd find at the beginning of a book about wisdom—that is, a nice, neat definition of what wisdom is—it's not here. We find from the start that this book resists neat ordering and packaging. And I would suggest from the start that we acknowl-edge the resistance and even enjoy it. The prologue provides the set of vocabulary that the book will unpack. But the words don't come in a neat list; they wind together, some repeating, as we follow the turns of the poetic lines. These verses let us begin to peer into the many facets of wisdom, to turn these words round and round in our minds sort of like a kaleidoscope. As a kaleidoscope enables us to glimpse the changing patterns of shapes and colors, so in Proverbs we glimpse the multi-faceted nature of wisdom lived in the flow of daily life. The point is that wisdom touches all of life, as its moments flow not in neatly organized categories but in the ever-changing complexity of human experience.

As Proverbs asks us to consider wisdom, it does not present a set of truths to learn and affirm. Rather, Proverbs points to wisdom that transforms all of life. That is why we will find Wisdom (or the **personification** of wisdom—we'll talk about that) in this book calling out from street corners and marketplaces, invading not just religious ceremonies but kitchens and bedrooms and places of business and barns and sheep pastures. Wisdom in this book is sticking her nose into every little nitty-gritty part of life. This can be challenging, but on the other hand, it can be immensely comforting. From whatever angle we look into whatever part of life, we need wisdom, and we can find wisdom. Kidner astutely communicates this truth, in probably his most quoted comment on Proverbs:

> "It is a book which seldom takes you to church. Like its own figure of Wisdom, it calls across to you in the street about some every-day matter, or points things out at home. Its function in Scripture is to put godliness into working clothes." (*Proverbs*, page 35)

Questions for reflection

1. What voices offering wisdom do you hear around you today? What kinds of wisdom are they offering?

2. If someone asked you how Proverbs fits into the Bible, what would you say?

3. As you read the prologue (v 1-7), what words or phrases stand out, and why? How do you initially respond to the call it contains?

PART TWO

Watching the Kaleidoscope Turn

Having acknowledged and even celebrated the complexity, we should note that there is order to be found in the book's opening lines. **Verses 2-4** work as a unit, with a steadily repeated pattern of in-finitives (the "to" form of the verbs, as in "to know" and "to under-stand," "to receive" and "to give"). Teachers often take these verses to summarize the book's aim: that is, to point the reader toward wis-dom in all its various aspects: *intellectual* in **verse 2** (knowing and un-derstanding); *ethical* in **verse 3** (wise dealing, righteousness, justice, equity); and *practical* in **verse 4** (prudence, knowledge, discretion). These multiple categories tell us that when we aim for wisdom, we aim for much more than an intellectual process. There is "instruction" in **verse 2** *and* in **verse 3**—for both the knowing and the doing. Ac-tually, as these lines flow together and the kaleidoscope turns, we see that the kind of knowing introduced here is a deep knowing: the kind that cannot be separated from living. Godly wisdom infuses a whole person and all of that person's character and life.

If **verses 2-4** summarize the book's aim in regard to wisdom, then **verses 5-6** drive home that aim with a call to pursue it and find its rewards. The first and crucial part of the call is indeed to *hear* (**v 5**). Proverbs will keep on driving home the point that hearing—listening humbly to wisdom's words—is the necessary means of seeking and finding wisdom. The rewards are of course multi-faceted, including not only an "increase in learning" but also more practical "guidance," for one who hears and understands these proverbs.

The audience to which this call to wisdom is addressed expands clearly and steadily through these lines. In **verse 4**, the receivers are "the simple" and "the youth"—which helps confirm the generally accepted understanding that this book was originally used for Israel's leaders-in-training. The word "simple" indicates someone naïve or untaught, as are many young people; these words work together. The call broadens, however, seeming to give a check to those who might read the first verses and assume that they are already wise and do not need this wisdom.

Proverbs' audience turns out to be as multi-faceted as wisdom itself. In **verse 5** the call extends to "the wise" and to "the one who understands," communicating the ongoing need to seek and apply wisdom—and the need for humility in the process in order to keep on listening. This is a book not just for youth; this wisdom is continually needed by all of us, young and old, male and female. I am included, and you are included, in the ones who need to stop and listen.

Verse 6 returns to the *understanding* introduced back in **verse 2** and reiterated in **verse 5**. The almost playful multiple terms seem to emphasize the complexity of rightly interpreting a "proverb," a "saying," "words of the wise," and "riddles." It seems a daunting task.

Even as we try to organize and categorize these weighty wisdom words, we do sense that they point to puzzles—"riddles" that will be hard to figure out. Many of the verses ahead will puzzle us! They cover breadths that are beyond us. Sometimes a kaleidoscope takes our breath away. We might think back to Solomon's wisdom and understanding "beyond measure." He spoke 3,000 proverbs and wrote 1,005 songs (1 Kings 4:32). He studied trees, "from the cedar that is in Lebanon to the hyssop that grows out of the wall," and beasts, and birds, and reptiles, and fish (1 Kings 4:33). God's world—both in nature and in human nature—contains layers and depths that the wisest of us readers will find impossible to grasp.

The concluding verse of the prologue will point us in the right direction in order to face this daunting task.

Wisdom in Relationship With the Lord

We've said that Proverbs' wisdom is not just learned intellectually but lived out practically. And it's not lived out alone. We're ready for the third observation: *Proverbs' wisdom is found in relationship with the*

Lord. From the rest of Scripture we know the primacy of relationship with the Lord God, so it should not surprise us to find it here in Proverbs. But it is important to see and say, especially because of the common temptation to think of Proverbs as a collection of sayings, rather than a book about relationship with God.

The more carefully we read this book, the more we see wisdom as a life lived in active relationship with God: listening, following, repenting—and, first and foremost here at the start, fearing. The prologue's climactic verse tells us, "The fear of the LORD is the beginning of knowledge" (Proverbs **1:7a**). Fearing God (a call found throughout the Old Testament) is different from just being afraid, as we would be afraid of a storm or a burglar. That kind of fear is flavored by objects which simply harm us. Right fear of God is flavored by its object as well: the Lord God of the universe, who has revealed himself in the Scriptures. Fearing the Lord means reverencing him for who he is, according to his word. Fearing him is the beginning: the starting point for all these weighty wisdom words. It's the thing that gets the kaleidoscope turning.

We should notice that the text does not say *the fear of God*. It says "the fear of the LORD"—*Yahweh*. (Bible translations often print this name all in capital letters.) This is God's revealed name for himself as the One who in steadfast love redeems a people for himself. Yes, this Lord is the sovereign Creator of all things. Yes, this Lord is the holy Judge of all people. The Lord God is one God. And yet *Yahweh* is a special name for God: it is the name God gave Moses to use in telling the people of Israel who it was that sent him to rescue them from Egypt: "Say this to the people of Israel: 'The LORD, the God of your fathers, the God of Abraham, the God of Isaac, and the God of Jacob, has sent me to you.' This is my name forever" (Exodus 3:15). The LORD is the One who mercifully rescues a sinful people according to his promises.

That rescue was first hinted at in the Garden of Eden, after the fall, when God promised that the seed of the woman would bruise the head of that serpent (Genesis 3:15). God channeled the rescue through Abraham and his seed, promising to bless them, to make them a great nation in the land he promised to give them, and through them to bring blessing to all the nations (Genesis 12:1-7). By the time of King Solomon, Abraham's seed that Yahweh rescued from Egypt had indeed become a great, prosperous nation, blessing all the nations around through the wisdom of their king. They were receiving the fruit of Yahweh's promises. And yet it was not the final fruit. We read the book of Proverbs today knowing about the kingdom of Israel, which flourished and then fell, as God's people turned away from their Lord.

> Proverbs is full of relationships—but there is no other starting point than a relationship with the Lord.

But the LORD's name is forever. His word does not fail. We also know that the LORD brought that promised seed to this world, according to his covenant. The seed came through the line of David and Solomon and their descendants, down through the line of Judah, all the way to Jesus. When we read the name of "the LORD" today, we sense the depths of that name as it has been revealed in history, and the depths of the love with which that name reverberates. This is the merciful God who redeems his people for himself, finally through his Son.

The beginning point of wisdom in Proverbs is the beginning point for all God's people throughout all time: we must fear the Lord. That is, we must reverence him for who he is according to his word. This is the relationship that determines everything. Proverbs is full of relationships (just like our lives): fathers and sons, mothers and sons, husbands and wives, men and women who are not husbands and wives, neighbors with each other, rulers and subjects, and on and on. But there is no other starting point than this relationship with the Lord whom we are called to fear. What grace that he reveals himself to us, and that he himself redeems us, so that we are able to fear him as his beloved redeemed people.

The fear of the Lord will be put before us again and again, at crucial points in the book. It is the only starting point for a life of wisdom, and it is the necessary continuing touchpoint all along wisdom's path.

Wisdom Versus Folly

But there is a second line of Proverbs **1:7**. The prologue comes to a climax not with one positive statement concerning the fear of the Lord, but with two parallel lines of poetry that set up a contrast and lead us to the fourth observation: *Proverbs' wisdom is the alternative to folly*:

"The fear of the LORD is the beginning of knowledge;
fools despise wisdom and instruction."

After all the build-up of those weighty wisdom words in the previous verses, after that compelling kaleidoscopic call to wisdom, and finally after the very name of the Lord and the call to fear him, that second line of this verse is like suddenly hitting a brick wall.

Here at the start of Proverbs, we are obviously meant to feel the dramatically deadly contrast between wisdom and folly. These two paths cut their way through all the wisdom literature, showing the two ways to live and the two destinations toward which they head. This verse makes it clear: there is the way of wisdom, which begins with the fear of the Lord, and there is the way of folly, in which wisdom is despised and rejected.

It's not just that fools do not *find* or *choose* wisdom; rather, they *despise* it. They *hate* it! These two lines actually set up an interesting antithetic parallelism. (We'll get into the details of the poetry later, but for now, we are noticing two paired lines that say quite opposite things; that's "antithetic parallelism.") Now, you might expect that the "fools" in line 2 would contrast directly with the "wise" in line 1. But there are no wise people in line 1. There is only the fear of the Lord. It is the Lord himself, and the fear of him, that these fools are set against. The fools reject that relationship; ultimately it is the Lord himself they despise.

It's a helpful truth to remember: people choosing the path of folly don't need just an argument; they need to meet a person. Proverbs calls us to that meeting.

After piling up all the benefits of wisdom, the prologue does not name the rewards of folly. Proverbs will get to those rewards in the course of its instruction; we will vividly confront wisdom's and folly's contrasting ends—essentially life and death. The prologue is a call to wisdom and to life. It does not take us down the other path; the dire contrast simply suggests the worst, in this ominous negative note that concludes an overwhelmingly positive opening call. The tension created by this final line pushes us ahead to grasp the import of the words that follow in verse 8: "Hear, my son, your father's *instruction*…" (emphasis mine). Fools despise that *instruction* (**v 7**)—the very *instruction* that Proverbs insistently calls us to receive (**v 2, 3**).

Christ Our Wisdom

We've said it multiple times, but let's reiterate it as the fifth and final observation: *Proverbs' wisdom stretches through God's revelation, revealed fully in Christ.* We will see suggestions and reverberations of this truth emerge throughout the book. The prologue itself points to this truth, not explicitly but implicitly.

The shape of the prologue points us outward and upward—in the opening, first, to the history of the kingdom of Israel, and in the end to the fear of Yahweh, the LORD, who made a covenant with Israel that stretched far into the future. From the start we are aware of God's people, through whom he declared that he would demonstrate wisdom, as we saw in Deuteronomy 4:6. It is this people who, throughout Scripture's big story so far, have been told repeatedly to fear the Lord—for example, in Deuteronomy 6:13: "It is the LORD your God you shall fear."

It's not a huge stretch to follow the trajectory of this people all the way through the story, as they repeatedly fail to fear the Lord and follow his laws. The Israelites did not show wisdom to the world as they were called to do. The fulfillment of God's promises to them arrived in the deliverer who came in their line—the Lord Jesus, in whom are hidden all the treasures of wisdom and knowledge (Colossians 2:3), the One whom the apostle Paul calls "wisdom from God" (1 Corinthians 1:24).

If it is true that our relationship with the Lord is at the heart of Proverbs, then readers of the whole Bible will actually have a hard time not connecting Proverbs with the promised Lord Jesus, who came to make such a relationship possible, through his death on our behalf and his resurrection from the dead. We might not be able to get out of our minds what Paul says about Scripture's sacred writings, "which are able to make you wise for salvation through faith in Christ Jesus" (2 Timothy 3:15).

As we move through Proverbs, we will want to hold this truth clearly and yet carefully in our minds, focusing first on the inspired text before us and hearing it with open ears, even as the original readers would have heard it. With care and humility, then, we will be ready to ask how these words bear witness to our Savior—even as he himself said that all the Scriptures do (John 5:39).

Jesus came to teach and show us wisdom in the fullest way. At the climax of the Sermon on the Mount in Matthew 7, for example, we should not be surprised to find a story about the wise man and the foolish man! And what was that story to teach us? Jesus explained, "Everyone then who hears these words of mine and does them will be like a wise man who built his house on the rock" (Matthew 7:24). Proverbs will call us to hear and follow wisdom's words: "Let the wise hear" (Proverbs **1:5**). As we open our ears to the wisdom of Proverbs—wisdom we all so desperately need—may that wisdom point us to the Lord Jesus.

Jesus is the full and final context of Proverbs' wisdom. In Jesus is the most dazzling, kaleidoscopic revelation of wisdom lived out. Jesus is the way to a relationship with God. Jesus exposes the deadly foolishness of the other way. Proverbs' wisdom stretches forward and bursts into full light in the person of Jesus.

Questions for reflection

1. Proverbs addresses multiple audiences. Which ones strike you as especially important?

2. "People choosing the path of folly don't need just an argument; they need to meet a person." How does Proverbs show that truth, and how have you witnessed it yourself?

3. Read 1 Corinthians 1:18-25, and comment on what you see about wisdom in relation to Jesus Christ.

2. VOICES OF WISDOM

We've heard the prologue calling us to wisdom and its fruit—and now Proverbs begins to develop that call. Part One of this chapter will take us through the rest of Proverbs 1, with a fatherly instruction and a personal address from Wisdom. We readers get to join the hearers. Part Two will look ahead to see how the pattern of wisdom teaching is now set for the book's first major section.

Hear, My Son

Proverbs' prologue in verses 1-7 gave an overwhelmingly positive call, ending with one sharp line of negative warning. An instruction immediately follows with a message that dramatically develops the negative. The structure of this teaching looks like this:

- Opening call to hear (**v 8-9**)

- Main instruction (**v 10**)

- Temptation not to hear (**v 11-14**)

- Reasons to hear (**v 15-18**)

- Concluding lesson (**v 19**)

The opening call to hear (**v 8a**) is key, not just for its continuation of the prologue's ringing call (v 5a) but also for its establishment of this call (or some version of it) as the opening of each instruction—and really as the central call of the book. Proverbs does not say, *Here, affirm this list of truths.* It says, *Hear these words that are coming to* *you live!* The setting is a warm, live one, in which a father and mother together are pictured as offering their son "instruction" and "teaching" (parallel words that give matching weight to the father's and the mother's guidance). The son's two possible responses are anticipated in the parallel commands: the positive command to "hear" and the negative command to "forsake not." True hearing in fact would mean not forsaking. In Proverbs, true hearing, like true knowing, is more than something that happens in a person's head. It always involves life-altering results, as words penetrate the heart and then transform actions.

> True hearing is more than something that happens in a person's head. It involves life-altering results.

The negative command dominates this instruction—but not before we see a quick flash of the reward for hearing and heeding it. Verse 9 holds out, just for a moment, an enticing picture of how blessed this son's life will be if he listens. The graceful garland and pendants bring to our imaginations concrete images of beauty and riches, along with connotations of success and favor. We will see such pictures again in Proverbs; they keep appearing and enticing us along wisdom's path, showing us that though the instruction might seem hard, the rewards are as wonderful as the most beautiful adornments and gems we can imagine.

This opening instruction is indeed hard. It always seems to me to be a startlingly quick descent into dark, sordid scenes, after such an exalted beginning to the book. The point must be to startle us with the depths of this folly, which stands in contrast to wisdom, whose heights soar by contrast. The point must be to make vividly clear from the start just what is at stake in this teaching: nothing less than life and death.

The kernel of the instruction comes in **verse 10**: "If sinners entice you, do not consent." In **verses 11-14**, the father gives a sample of the sinners' enticing voices, which try to persuade the son to hear and follow them. (It becomes clear that, although the mother is repeatedly mentioned in Proverbs, the father is the primary one speaking in these instructions, addressing "my son"; see for example Proverbs 4:3.) Through the violent words he attributes to these sinners, the father shows their vicious cruelty: they would "lie in wait for blood" and "ambush the innocent without reason" (**1:11**). They actually compare themselves to Sheol, the place of the dead or the grave, as they aim to swallow alive these innocent people they would plunder. At the very same time they promise overflowing wealth for all who will join them.

The father resumes speaking in his own voice in **verse 15** (with another "my son"), as he proceeds to explain the folly of being taken in by such voices. In his explanation he uses an image, a picture—one that Proverbs will show us again and again. When the father says, "Do not walk in the way with them," and "Hold back your foot from their paths," the picture of a path is planted in our minds—here a path on which the son must not walk, along with such companions.

The picture of the path will recur and grow in meaning. In this passage, the father's point is that the sinners' path is a way of "evil," along which these men are not just walking but running (**v 16**). The imagery develops as the men are compared in **verse 17** to birds, which, as they fly along their way, are aware enough not to fly into a net that they see someone spreading in front of them; these men, by ironic contrast, are so foolish that on their path, as we picture it, they are in effect setting an ambush for themselves. They think they lie in wait for the blood of others (**v 11a**); actually, they "lie in wait for their own blood" (**v 18a**). In later sections Proverbs will make vivid the ways in which cruelty and violence destroy the lives not just of others but finally of the perpetrators themselves.

The instruction's conclusion (**v 19**) draws out this image into a larger lesson: "Such are the ways" of people who seek "unjust gain." We have been given a picture of a path of sin that leads to destruction:

a direction of heart and action that takes away life. As we hear this teaching, we should remember that the prologue called to a larger audience than immature youths; it called to "the wise" and "the one who understands" (v 5). And we might understand already that this initial instruction, although it clearly warns youths against joining gangs of looters, in a larger sense warns us all against the enticement of seeking reward along the wrong path.

Most basically it warns against listening to the wrong voice. We have noted the personal setting here, with live words addressed by a father to his son and then imagined words addressed by sinners to that son. We have said that Proverbs is not about rules but about a relationship: one in which we are called to listen to words—ultimately God's words. And so it makes sense that we are thrust into scenarios where words are being offered in the context of various relationships. The question is: Whose words will we hear? The next section will tell us Proverbs' answer to that question.

Wisdom Introduced

Before we actually hear Wisdom we are first introduced to her, in **verses 20-21**. In this scene (and in several others) Proverbs pictures wisdom as a person: a woman named Wisdom. (In discussions of such passages, the name Wisdom is often capitalized.) We have already glimpsed the imagery, or the picture-language, at work in this poetic literature. The kind of imagery we find in this case is personification: a figure of speech in which something nonhuman is pictured as though it were a person—such as when trees clap their hands (Isaiah 55:12) or when righteousness and peace kiss each other (Psalm 85:10). We know we're just pretending with these pictures, but the pictures let us imagine in a way that shows us truth.

The picture of wisdom as a woman has been much discussed, among all sorts of commentators and critics. Who is this woman? Why a *woman*? Is this a portrait of the female gender as the embodiment of wisdom? Is this a kind of goddess figure? Or is this a sexist portrayal of a woman as the prize to seek, in an ancient training manual for men? Or, if we make the kinds of whole-Bible connections with Christ that we have already suggested, will we get into trouble by imposing on Jesus a female identity?

Some point out that it makes perfect sense in context that wisdom should be pictured here as a woman. We've noted the addresses to "my son," and we've discussed the early use of Proverbs to train young leaders in Israel—which would have been young *men* in Israel—and so it might seem reasonable to picture the wisdom to be sought in terms of a woman to be pursued. Actually, although a female figure certainly would have attracted young men's attention, Wisdom does not play the role of a woman trying to attract a man in a romantic or gender-related way; she is bigger than that, calling youth and calling all to listen and follow her because, as we will hear, life and death are at stake.

The commentator Bruce Waltke refers us to a tradition of scholarship that relates to this female figure: languages with masculine and feminine **nouns** have usually followed that gender distinction in poetic language, including personifications. "The abstract noun *hokmâ* [*wisdom* in Hebrew] is feminine and accordingly becomes personified as a woman" (*The Book of Proverbs Chapters 1 – 15*, page 83). The Hebrew noun for "folly" is also feminine, and we shall meet the woman named Folly later on, in chapter 9.

Understanding the imagery is fundamental to understanding Wisdom. Proverbs is not telling us that wisdom itself is female; no, Proverbs is picturing, or personifying, wisdom as a woman. In Psalm 19 the sun is pictured as a bridegroom and as a strong man, and no one is worried that we're going to get the sun confused with a man! The best way to understand this Wisdom is to look at the picture closely. What is this woman like? What is she doing? What does this tell us about wisdom? The prologue has introduced us to wisdom in all its complexity and beauty; now in the figure of this woman we get to peer into a live picture of it. We will look closely—first here in Proverbs 1 where we meet Wisdom, and then especially later in chapters 8 and 9, where the imagery climaxes in a powerful way.

Wisdom is introduced straight after the father's first instruction, and she gives a similar warning and promise. Her words, however, echo in a larger way, for Wisdom does not speak here in an intimate family scene but calls out in the most public context. Four parallel verbs emphasize her words for all to hear: "cries aloud," "raises her voice" (**1:20**), "cries out," and "speaks" (**v 21**). And four settings light up the parts of a city where all sorts of people would gather for the main activities of life: "the street" where they live and "the markets" where they buy and sell (**v 20**); "the head of the noisy streets" where everybody can see and hear and "the entrance of the city gates" where civic leaders would make decisions (**v 21**). Kaleidoscopic wisdom has come to life!

Wisdom Calling

After Wisdom is introduced, she speaks (**v 22-33**). Her predominantly negative warning is laced with a quick flash of positive promise, as a brief outline suggests:

- Opening reproach (**v 22**)

- Promise for those who will hear (**v 23**)

- Warning for those who refuse to hear (**v 24-31**)

- Summary teaching: two ways and two ends (**v 32-33**)

The opening (**v 22**) addresses three categories of people along the path of foolishness: the "simple" (the naïve or immature, as we saw in the prologue); the "scoffers" (fools that stand out, "delighting" in their scoffing); and "fools" in general, who (as in v 7) "hate knowledge." Wisdom doesn't start out by simply condemning them; she mixes condemnation with a yearning for their foolishness to end, repeating those words, "How long?"

Wisdom's opening here reminds me of God's words calling to Israel through his prophet Jeremiah:

"O Jerusalem, wash your heart from evil,
    that you may be saved.

> *How long* shall your wicked thoughts
>> lodge within you?" (Jeremiah 4:14, emphasis mine; see also
>>> Numbers 14:11, 27; Hosea 8:5)

Wisdom's next words offer a promise that rings out even more strikingly: if these people will "turn" to her when she rebukes them, then, she says: "I will pour out my spirit to you; / I will make my words known to you" (Proverbs **1:23**). Many point out the resonance between this verse and the similarly worded promise in Joel 2:28-9 (see also Isaiah 32:15). The New Testament picks up these promises—most notably in Acts 2:17, as the apostle Peter quotes the prophet Joel to explain the outpouring of the Holy Spirit at Pentecost.

Before we draw any conclusions from these biblical resonances that seem to jump out at us, let's take a brief look at the rest of Wisdom's call. We've seen her heart to reclaim the foolish; next we see her substantive warning concerning those who refuse to listen.

The warning in Proverbs **1:24-31** consists of two extended *because/therefore* sections. The first (**v 24-28**) focuses on what Wisdom has done and how people have responded—and how therefore she will in the end respond to them. She has called and she has stretched out her hand, and they have refused to listen (**v 24**; see **v 25**); therefore ("therefore" is implied at the start of **v 26**) when calamity and terror come on them and they call to her, she will not answer (**v 26-28**). In fact, she will laugh at their distress. One cannot help but think of the similarly startling picture in Psalm 2:4 of God in the heavens laughing—holding in derision those earthly kings who set themselves against him.

The second *because/therefore* section repeats much of the first but focuses more on the foolish ones themselves—and adds a significant phrase, one which lights up all the phrases around it. Proverbs **1:29b** tells us that they "did not choose the fear of the LORD." Interestingly, **verse 30** goes on to repeat **verse 25** almost exactly: the foolish reject Wisdom's counsel and despise her reproof. And yet, in light of the interjection of **verse 29**, we understand that rejecting Wisdom's counsel and reproof means rejecting the fear of the Lord. Listening to Wisdom here is identified directly with fearing the Lord.

The final two verses of her speech clarify the message: Wisdom's words are the key. Turn away from her call and be destroyed (**v 32**), or be someone who "listens to me" and who "will dwell secure" (**v 33**).

What shall we conclude at this point about this personification of wisdom? Here is one way to say it: this woman brings us a living picture of the very words of God. Often she sounds like one of God's prophets—those who spoke the very words of God. Actually, when she speaks, it sounds a lot like God speaking! Her call goes out for all to hear. She promises her spirit and in mercy reaches out her hand. She warns of judgment. She says her words can turn people from death to life. To be clear, this Wisdom is not an actual appearance of a prophetess or of God or Jesus or *anybody*; this is a poetic picture that enlivens our imaginations and hearts to hear the very voice of God in his revelation to us.

Wisdom's voice helps us grasp how God, through his word, mercifully speaks into the lives (every part of the lives) of human beings. Wisdom's voice helps us understand God's love and desire for us to turn to him, and his grace in pouring out his Spirit on us when we repent and believe his word. Wisdom's voice warns us of God's condemnation of sin and the coming judgment when it will be too late to repent. Wisdom's voice reminds us that hearing and following God's word is not a matter of being happier but a matter of life and death: eternal security versus eternal destruction. To "dwell secure" (**v 33a**) implies being safe at home and staying there.

We will see more of Wisdom. This is only the start. It's a start that helps us understand Proverbs' call to hear—and to begin that hearing with the fear of the Lord who reveals himself in his word.

Questions for reflection

1. Why do you think Proverbs spends so much time showing us folly's path?

2. Was there a time when God's word called you from the path of folly, or a time when you were able to give a call to someone heading down that path?

3. Respond to this woman Wisdom! Summarize what you see her showing us about God.

PART TWO

Getting the Shape of the Book

In Proverbs 1, the father's instruction and Wisdom's call establish a pattern of wisdom teaching that extends through to the end of Proverbs 9. This wisdom teaching can be organized in various ways, but many agree that there are ten main instructions that begin with "My son." The instructions are interspersed with several wisdom sections: an address by Wisdom (as we have just seen), or a poem about wisdom (as we will see in chapter 3), or another kind of passage on wisdom. After the prologue, chapters 1 – 9 make up the first main section of the book, which might be outlined as follows (these divisions agree with those in the ESV Study Bible; see also Wilson, *Proverbs: An Introduction and Commentary*, page 12):

- Instruction 1 (**1:8-19**)
    - Wisdom section 1 (**1:20-33**)
- Instruction 2 (**2:1-22**)
- Instruction 3 (**3:1-12**)
    - Wisdom section 2 (**3:13-20**)
- Instruction 4 (**3:21-35**)
- Instruction 5 (4:1-9)
- Instruction 6 (4:10-19)
- Instruction 7 (4:20-27)
- Instruction 8 (5:1-23)
    - Wisdom section 3 (6:1-19)
- Instruction 9 (6:20-35)
- Instruction 10 (7:1-27)
    - Wisdom section 4 (8:1-36)
    - Wisdom section 5 (9:1-18)

This first large section of wisdom teaching comes first in the book for a reason! When we think of Proverbs, what often comes first to mind is the collection of actual proverbs: those short sayings that begin in chapter 10 and fill most of the remaining chapters. And we often dive too quickly into those proverbs, without first establishing the foundation for them that Proverbs establishes in chapters 1 – 9.

Aren't we all somewhat tempted just to jump in, start grabbing those nuggets of wisdom, and get on with living happier and more virtuous lives? In many ways, the proverbs starting in chapter 10 are a lot more snappy and fun than the longer poetic passages in chapters 1 – 9. Maybe, we might think, we could begin by taking one proverb a day, kind of like vitamins, and surely our days would get better and better. They might! But here's the catch: if we don't begin as this book leads us to begin, then we're likely to end up not really knowing what to do with the proverbs, and we'll most likely be frustrated because they're not working.

What will we do, for example, with the famous and seemingly contradictory couple of proverbs in chapter 26?

"Answer not a fool according to his folly,
  lest you be like him yourself.
Answer a fool according to his folly,
  lest he be wise in his own eyes." (26:4-5)

A proverb cannot change our life. Two proverbs may just confuse us. Obviously we have to know how to apply the proverbs in a variety of circumstances. But how can we know? We may just end up showing the truth of 26:7: "Like a lame man's legs, which hang useless, / is a proverb in the mouth of fools."

What's the solution? We have to find wisdom first. We have to be listening to Wisdom's voice—that is, God's voice. We have to begin with the fear of the Lord, or we'll get nowhere with the proverbs. That is why Proverbs begins with its first nine chapters. We need to turn from folly and learn wisdom in relationship with the Lord, fearing him as he reveals himself in his word. Living in that relationship, we'll be ready to follow wisdom along all the twists and turns of life's path, because it will be the path that leads to life as opposed to death.

We will make our way rather quickly through these first nine chapters, but hopefully with enough attention to see how they prepare us to take in the proverbs to come. The big point has already been made, and now it is further developed: to find wisdom we must listen, and that listening begins with the fear of the Lord.

Following Instructions

Three questions will help guide us through the next three instructions (instructions 2, 3, and 4). We'll begin in some detail with the second instruction, and the others follow in briefer form.

Instruction 2 (2:1-22)

1. What is the structure of this teaching?

A simple outline will help:

- IF (**v 1-4**)

- THEN/FOR (**v 5-8**)

- THEN/FOR (**v 9-15**)

- SO/FOR (**v 16-19**)

- SO/FOR (**v 20-22**)

This is not the only possible way to divide up this instruction. But it is one that works—by following the connecting words that provide logical transitions in these flowing passages of poetry. Let me explain.

Verses 1-4 give three "if's," setting up a condition for the whole of the rest of the poem. The father is saying, *If you open your heart wide to wisdom...* He calls his son to receive his words because he is offering himself as a spokesman for the teaching of God's word (which is the role of a parent, according to Deuteronomy 6:1-9). Proverbs **2:1-4** is a passage worthy of prayerful **meditation**: How well do I receive words of wisdom from God, treasuring them in my heart (**v 1**)? What does it mean to make my ear attentive and incline my heart (**v 2**)? Do I seek wisdom and understanding like silver, like the most valuable hidden treasures (**v 4**)?

After the "if" come two "then's": these indicate two results that will occur *if* the condition is met. The first is amazing, especially considering what Proverbs has told us so far: "Then you will understand the fear of the LORD / and find the knowledge of God" (**v 5**). We can understand the fear of the Lord! This is not an elusive mystery. If we seek wisdom, we will find wisdom. Why? Here's the accompanying "for" (**v 6**): "For the LORD gives wisdom; / from his mouth come knowledge and understanding." Here is the plain, beautiful truth: this wisdom is from God, who gives it to us through his word—and not only that, but he becomes our shield, watching over us as his own (**v 7-8**).

The second "then" begins with the same words: "Then you will understand…" (**v 9**). Verses 9-15 describe the process of wisdom coming into our heart and soul, transforming our understanding and our actions. We will then be guarded by discretion and delivered from those given to evil, who are walking not on wisdom's paths but on crooked ones.

After the two results come the "so's"—or the two conclusions: one more specific and negative, one more general and positive. The more specific conclusion (**v 16-19**) is another deliverance: from "the forbidden woman" (**v 16**) a figure we will meet again. Two heartbreaking lines describe her as an adulteress "who forsakes the companion of her youth / and forgets the **covenant** of her God" (**v 17**). The son who seeks wisdom will be delivered from her, "for her house sinks down to death" (**v 18**).

The final "so" pictures the son walking in "the way of the good" and "the paths of the righteous" (**v 20**). The concluding "for" (**v 21-22**) summarizes the two ways: that of the upright, who will inhabit and remain in the land, and that of the wicked, who will be cut off from the land. The first instruction concluded with a promise of dwelling secure (**1:33**); here again comes the assurance of a safe place in which to live and remain, in this promised land.

2. What is the key idea of this instruction?

Rereading the passage and reviewing our outline, we find the key idea to be that the Lord gives treasures of wisdom through his word, if we open our ears and our hearts. This is an overwhelmingly encouraging instruction.

Again the fear of the Lord is explicitly before us in the text, reminding us that all these treasures flow from a relationship with him, in which we reverence him for who he is according to his word—and then as we walk forward in the security of that relationship.

3. How are the two paths, of wisdom and folly, made vivid in this instruction? And how are we drawn to walk on wisdom's path?

The father's instructions illumine the two ways, by not just describing them but urging his son to reject one and walk in the other. In this second instruction, the path of wisdom is described as protected and pleasant, leading to a place of permanent security—contrasting with the crooked path, where evil men and women are sinking down to death. Listening, we see and recoil from that deadly path and are drawn toward the path of life. This is a heartening instruction, pulling us forward and letting us sense the gracious call of God the Father in this father's words.

> The path of wisdom is protected and pleasant, leading to a place of permanent security.

In short, if the message of the first instruction was to stay off the bad guys' path, the message of this one is to seek the good path.

Instruction 3 (3:1-12)

1. What is the structure?

Six commands here flesh out what it means to fear the Lord. Each command is linked to a motivation or reward for obeying that command.

How delightful that Proverbs likes to make lists of things—it helps us get it straight!

As you observe this list, notice how the progression of commands focuses in the very center on the fear of the Lord (**3:7b**), and moves in the end toward the reward of a relationship with the Lord himself as our loving Father who disciplines us because he delights in us (**v 12**).

2. What is the key idea?

Fearing the Lord involves a life of obeying his word—and brings a life overflowing with his love and blessing.

3. How are the two paths made vivid?

This instruction peers almost completely down the good path, with hints of the path of folly that would involve turning away from the word of the Lord; we feel the implicit warning here.

Our hearts are pulled by the promises: blessings overflow along the path of learning to trust and obey the word of the Lord: that is, walking in fear of him. Will our barns always be filled with plenty (**v 10a**)? Reading all the proverbs, we will find the answer to be "no." For now, we can observe a trustworthy pattern of God's good hand (including his hand of discipline in **v 11-12**) on those who know the blessing of living in relationship with him.

In short, if the message of the first instruction was to stay off the bad guys' path, and the message of the second was to seek the good path, then the message of this third instruction is to walk this path obediently—and find the Lord's presence and blessing along the way.

Instruction 4 (3:21-35)

1. What is the structure?

- Initial call: Keep on wisdom's path of life (**v 21-24**)
- Six things NOT to do along the path (**v 25-31**)
- Four final contrasts that keep us motivated along wisdom's path (**v 32-35**)

2. What is the key idea?

We will be tempted to disobey along wisdom's path; *don't* disobey, but rather persevere in fearing the Lord and following his word.

This instruction is more negative; it acknowledges the need to persevere along the way, as we are tempted to lose sight of wisdom up ahead calling us. We easily become fearful of other things around us, rather than persisting in fear of the Lord.

3. How are the two paths made vivid?

This instruction tells us to keep the stuff from the bad path off of the good path; it doesn't belong there! The big picture of where we are and where we're headed helps us order our steps along the way. The conclusion again motivates our obedience with the promise of a blessed dwelling: the inheritance of honor (received by the wise) as opposed to disgrace (received by fools).

This instruction will encourage any of us who need a reminder and motivation to persevere as we follow the Lord, which I guess would be all of us! I appreciate this instruction as a person who has known the Lord for a long time and who needs this call to keep walking faithfully to the end, not giving in to fears or foibles that would pull me off course.

In short, if the message of the first instruction was to stay off the bad guys' path; the message of the second was to seek the good path; and the message of the third was to walk this path obediently—finding blessing along the way; then the message of this fourth instruction is to keep on this path to the end, not losing our way.

The path of wisdom, and the foundation of wisdom this book establishes, is becoming ever more clear.

The Blessing of Wisdom

We've saved the best part for last. The wisdom section between the instructions in chapter 3 is one of Proverbs' most lovely (and important) passages. It is known as a "hymn to wisdom" because the poetry sings the blessings of those who find it—or *her*, we should say, as again we meet this personification of wisdom. This time, though, she is not speaking as a character but rather is being spoken about.

The key word is "blessed," introducing the main idea in **verse 13** and concluding the main body of the poem in **verse 18**. This hymn has been called an Old Testament **beatitude**, similar to the beatitudes Jesus spoke in Matthew 5:2-11, expressing what some call happiness and yet is in fact an even deeper well-being in one's soul. Waltke says that the sages reserved the term "blessed" for "people who experience life optimally, as the Creator intended" (*The Book of Proverbs Chapters 1 – 15*, page 256).

The best way to take in this poem about wisdom is to read and relish it out loud multiple times. After the introduction of Proverbs **3:13**, two verses express wisdom's worth (**v 14-15**), and two verses tell her benefits (**v 16-18**). Her worth is immeasurable; it can be expressed only through imagery, by comparison with the most valuable earthly treasures: silver, gold, jewels (**v 14-15**; recall 2:4). These are all most highly valued, but "nothing you desire can compare with her" (**3:15**).

Her benefits include riches and honor, but first, in her right hand, long life—life described in **3:17** as ways of pleasantness and paths of peace. The image of the tree of life in **verse 18** pulls our thoughts ahead to eternal life. Genesis 3:24 tells us that after they sinned, Adam and Eve were cut off from the tree of life in the Garden of Eden; now, wisdom comes and in herself brings that tree close so that people who will can reach out and lay hold of her, and be blessed with life forever.

This poem offers layers of pictures, pictures pointing us to divine mercy that restores life to sinful human beings who have broken their relationship with their Creator and so have been judged with death. The pictures grow in the concluding verses (Proverbs **3:19-20**), where we read that by wisdom the Lord created the earth: images of creation combine with some of those weighty wisdom words, in awesome and revealing ways.

We will have further glimpses of wisdom in this awesome role as the agent of creation and the source of eternal life. But even at this point our thoughts turn to Jesus, through whom and for whom all things were created (Colossians 1:16). He is the merciful Savior who came close and made it possible for us to be reconciled with our Creator, through his death on our behalf and his resurrection from the dead. By laying hold of him in faith, we do find eternal life, and paths of peace with God—the greatest blessedness.

We will meet many promises of blessing in Proverbs, and many of those blessings will be offered in terms of physical treasures—long life, successful profits, jewels, and so on. Those are treasures indeed, and gifts from God. But we will want to remember this passage and others that hold up such treasures in order to picture even more, and to tell us that nothing, even the most valuable things of this world, can compare with the blessing of wisdom.

Questions for reflection

1. The father keeps giving the call to "hear" instruction. What is involved in truly hearing God's word? How can we do it better?

2. What kind of a heart makes for peaceful sleep at night, and no fear of bad things coming at us (see Proverbs 3:24-25)?

3. How do wisdom's rewards make you think of Jesus?

3. TWO PATHS

The instructions continue in chapters 4 to 6, with wisdom's themes winding their way deep and deeper into the listener's mind and heart. This chapter's first part unfolds Proverbs 4, with its three further instructions that drive home the call to wisdom's path (in contrast to folly's). The second part addresses the various warnings against folly in Proverbs 5 – 6, framed with spotlights of instruction on the folly of adultery.

Are We Getting It?

We might think we've got the point by now. We have heard the insistent call to follow wisdom rather than folly—a call given in the voice not only of a wise father but also of Wisdom herself. But in his wisdom God our Father knows how slow we are to remember this call, and how quickly we turn aside or turn back. The further instructions in chapter 4 sound like those of parents who not only repeat themselves to make sure their children get it, but who also add some extra emphasis—some urging to think it over again and from this other angle...

When our boys were young, I would tell them to use the side door into the house if their feet were muddy. But of course I elaborated, especially when they forgot: "Not the *front* door, the *side* door. Why would you want to track mud into the front hallway? And think: if you wipe your feet on the outside mat, you will bring in less mud. And of course take your shoes off once you're inside." And so on.

Proverbs' instructions so far (four of them, in Proverbs 1 – 3) all began with a father's call to "my son," urging him to hear/receive/keep his words of wisdom. The general pattern continues in Proverbs 4, with each new instruction opening with the father's naming of the *son* and insistence on *hearing his instruction* (**4:1**), *hearing and accepting his words* (**v 10**), and *being attentive to his words* (**v 20**). Not only is the content of the instruction being planted deep in us, but also the example of consistent parental teaching as a channel of God's wisdom.

This example resonates with a larger scriptural call for families to pass on God's word to younger generations. As the Lord gave his people his laws, he commanded, "You shall teach them diligently to your children, and shall talk of them when you sit in your house, and when you walk by the way, and when you lie down, and when you rise" (Deuteronomy 6:7). This principle is highlighted even in the failure of parents to live it out—as in the sad example of Eli the priest and God's punishment on his house "because his sons were blaspheming God, and he did not restrain them" (1 Samuel 3:13). Many psalms declare the goodness of passing on God's truth: "One generation shall commend your works to another, / and shall declare your mighty acts" (Psalm 145:4). Many generations later, Pastor Timothy experienced this goodness: the apostle Paul speaks of Timothy's "sincere faith, a faith that dwelt first in your grandmother Lois and your mother Eunice, and now, I am sure, dwells in you as well" (2 Timothy 1:5).

Proverbs' instructions do serve the larger purpose of teaching wisdom to all; we must remember the breadth of the audience called out in the prologue. Every one of us readers needs to think of ourselves in the position of the "son" in Proverbs' early chapters, humbly receiving instruction that calls us away from folly and onto the path of the fear of the Lord. At the same time, however, as we take in these repeated portrayals of the father speaking and the son listening, we grasp the importance and beauty of this particular channel, from one generation to another.

I recall my father telling me, after the birth of my first son, that I was holding in my arms one of the greatest opportunities for evangelism that I would ever find. I've never forgotten those wise words.

Many books today address the problem of young people leaving the church. No simple solution to that problem exists. And yet here in Proverbs is a most basic starting point: the wise, consistent (even insistent) teaching passed on with loving care from one generation to the next. Whether we're mothers or fathers, aunts or uncles, teachers or friends, all of us believers who have been blessed by the teaching of others must consider how we can help pass on God's word to younger generations in God's family.

Instruction 5: The Intergenerational Path

The fifth instruction (Proverbs **4:1-9**) is one of my favorites, because it is so personal—and because it has a grandpa and a grandma in it! The key idea is this: *Listen well to this advice to pursue wisdom, for it came from my parents before me.* In fact, the bulk of the instruction (**v 4b-9**) is actually a long quotation that the father remembers receiving "when I was a son with my father, / tender, the only one in the sight of my mother" (**v 3**). The address to "sons," plural (**v 1a**), may draw out the sense of passing this generational wisdom on to many.

This instruction brings together many of the weighty wisdom words we have seen from the beginning of the book, showing a consistent call as the instruction is passed on. There is a double layer of the call to listen—both from the father in **verse 1** and again from the father's father in **verse 4**. The quoted words have an insistent theme: *get* wisdom and insight! The "get" comes twice in **verse 5** and twice in **verse 7**. Clearly, the call is to seek after this wisdom above all else and with all the energy of one's being, to the end.

But this is no ruthless search to procure something. Each double-pronged call to "get" is followed by counsel for the heart of the seeker after wisdom. In **verse 6b** comes the call to "love her," and **verse 8a** exhorts the son to "prize her highly." Again we find a relationship, as wisdom momentarily assumes the form of a woman who is to be loved and valued by one who cherishes and delights in her. We said earlier that the personification called Wisdom brings us a living picture of the very words of God. To love this wisdom is to be like the psalmist who cries out, "Oh how I love your law! / It is my meditation all the day" (Psalm 119:97), for "the law of your mouth is better to me / than thousands of gold and silver pieces" (Psalm 119:72).

Each double-pronged "get" also comes with promise of reward. Proverbs **4:6**: she will "keep" and "guard" you. **Verse 8**: she will "exalt" and "honor" you. The climactic promise in **verse 9** brings back the pictures from the first instruction (see 1:9): "She will place on your head a graceful garland; / she will bestow on you a beautiful crown."

Instruction 6: The Two Paths

Whereas the fifth instruction focuses on the call to wisdom, the sixth re-establishes the contrast between wisdom and folly. Again the father uses pictures of pathways to make vivid the life and death at stake. The structure here is as clear as the paths themselves: four verses lay out the "path of uprightness" (**4:10-13**); four verses lay out the "path of the wicked" (**v 14-17**); then two concluding verses give a final contrast (**v 18-19**).

Two things stand out in the descriptions of each path. The path of wisdom, first, is clearly presented as a path of *life*—as we see in both **verse 10** and **verse 13**. In **verse 10**, "your life" is made up of many years; by **verse 13**, "your life" has come to life in the figure of this instruction, which is to be sought, held onto, and guarded: "she *is* your life" (my emphasis). Again we find not an abstract quality to seek, but a relationship in which to live.

Second, on this good path the life is one of freedom. The path's boundaries create not limitations but security and strength—we can run with abandon: "When you walk, your step will not be hampered, / and if you run, you will not stumble" (**v 12**). Again we might hear echoes of Psalm 119: "I will run in the way of your commandments / when you enlarge my heart!" (Psalm 119:32). We will see these concepts fleshed out in the maxims to come; for example, specific proverbs about true versus false words will communicate the freeing, life-giving power of truth, and the destructive power of lies. But here in Proverbs' opening chapters, the way is laid and the concepts are clarified; above all, the call to wisdom rings out.

The entrance to the path of the wicked is cluttered with warning signs: "Do not enter" (Proverbs **4:14a**); "Do not walk" (**v 14b**); "Avoid it"and "Do not go on it"; "Turn away from it and pass on" (**v 15**).

Two awful descriptions reveal the experience of those who are on this path. First, "they cannot sleep unless they have done wrong" (**v 16a**). If we don't immediately grasp the horror of this, we're offered another chance, in even more distressing detail: "They are robbed of sleep unless they have made someone stumble" (**v 16b**). Most of us know the normal working of our consciences, which won't let us sleep when we have done wrong. How stunning to see the complete inversion of a healthy conscience, such that in order to sleep, one needs to have done wrong—and not just wrong in general but wrong that hurts another, causing another to stumble.

The second description here also offers a sickening reversal; rather than the actual bread and wine of a healthy, life-giving meal, the wicked "eat the bread of wickedness / and drink the wine of violence" (**v 17**). The perversion has become the normal thing, the desired thing, even the celebrated thing. What an apt description of the way evil works: to this day, it transforms sinful acts from shocking unnaturalness into the normal stuff of daily life.

> This is how evil works: it transforms sin from shocking unnaturalness into the normal stuff of daily life.

The final two verses of this instruction masterfully communicate the contrast through two quickly drawn images of light and dark. **Verse 18** shows the path of the righteous as the light of dawn: that is, as the second line explains, it is growing brighter and brighter as full day approaches. This is a picture of hope, of a path moving toward full life—life with no darkness at all.

By contrast, **verse 19** shows the way of the wicked as simply deep darkness. There is no change, no hope, no life. Those on that path can't even see what they're stumbling over (ironically, given that they take pleasure in causing others to stumble; see **v 16**).

Instruction 7: The Straight Path

The instruction that closes chapter 4 gives a call to take in deeply the words of wisdom (**v 20-23**), and then to let the life-giving effects flow outward in words and actions (**v 24-27**). In the first half, the son is urged to incline his ear to wisdom's words, focus on them with his eyes—and "keep them within your heart" (**v 21**). They are to be taken in deep; the *heart* focus is set in this verse and explained in **verse 23**: "Keep your heart with all vigilance, / for from it flow the springs of life."

These instructions keep turning us to the foundation of wisdom that must be established for us to deal rightly with the proverbs to come. We've seen that this wisdom begins with the fear of the Lord, which is not first a matter of actions but of a heart attitude. Fearing him means reverencing him for who he is and taking in his words humbly and deeply.

The repetition of the command to "keep" these words and "keep" our hearts implies a continual meditative focus on wisdom's instruction. We must not be like the person James describes, who sees his face in a mirror but "goes away and at once forgets what he was like" (James 1:23-24). Rather, we're to be like the one who "looks into the perfect law, the law of liberty, and perseveres, being no hearer who forgets but a doer who acts" (James 1:25).

As James makes clear, planting the word deep brings outward results, flowing from within. Proverbs also makes this clear. Proverbs **4:23** is a pivot verse, turning the flow from inward to outward, as springs of life flow from a heart where wisdom has been carefully kept. Those springs direct a person's words and actions—keeping them straight, we might say. On the good path there must be found no "crooked speech" or "devious talk" (**v 24**). The eyes of the one walking this path must "look directly forward," with a gaze "straight before you" (**v 25**). *Don't just wander mindlessly, but "ponder the path of your feet,"* says the instruction—so that your footsteps will "not swerve to the right or to the left" (**v 27**).

What prayers these verses should prompt us to pray, especially for young people around us! *Lord, by your grace, plant your word deep in her heart, and let the overflow from her mouth be life-giving and true. Lord, please keep him looking straight ahead, into the face of Jesus, who goes before us; let his gaze not be drawn aside. Lord, help her walk the good path, not swerving to the right or to the left, but drawn ahead by your voice as she hears—and ponders—your words in her heart.*

Questions for reflection

1. What wise people (parents or others) has God used to instruct you in wisdom? How did they do it?

2. To what young or less experienced ones (your children or other people) are you passing on God's wisdom? How do these passages encourage you?

3. What truths from Proverbs 4 can help keep us from getting moralistic and legalistic about walking the path of wisdom?

PART TWO

The Folly of the Forbidden Woman

After an instruction pointing ahead to wisdom's straight path, we stop to peer down the other path—the path of the wicked. On that path we find a woman who dominates the final three instructions. We were introduced to her in Proverbs 2:16: the "forbidden woman," also called "the adulteress with her smooth words." She reappears dramatically in chapter 5—again she is called the "forbidden woman" (**5:3**), which is sometimes translated the "strange" or "foreign" woman. She is consistently identified as an adulteress: that is, a married woman who is being unfaithful to her husband (see also **5:20**; **6:24, 26, 29**; 7:19).

Before delving into the warnings relating to this woman, we should ask why Proverbs' first section lands with such focus on her and on the evil of adultery that she represents. Considering all the kinds of foolishness and wisdom that Proverbs addresses, why is this one so central here, in the book's introductory section?

Our minds might first turn to the fact that sexual temptation is and always has been so strong and so disruptive in human relationships. In a book used at least partly and originally for the training of young men, sexual purity would naturally be a central issue to address. Indeed, for male and female alike, our gender and sexuality are at the core of our identity; to mess with God's order in this area is to mess up the foundation of our Creator's plan for human life that reflects and glorifies him.

That last statement connects sexual purity to something bigger than itself—and Proverbs leads us to do that. If the issue were limited to staying away from adulteresses, it would be crucial, but it might lack the larger resonance that we have sensed in Proverbs' wisdom from the prologue onward—with wisdom's kaleidoscopic beauty, its reaching out to a universal audience, and its connection to a relationship with the Lord God.

Proverbs' call to keep away from the adulteress is certainly a call for men to keep the marriage bed pure. Many have suggested that women can apply the same principle in reverse, so to speak, rejecting adulterous men; that suggestion surely helps enlarge the message. But the specific focus on the context of marriage (as opposed to other contexts of sexual sin) must lead us to consider what is at stake here: that is, the relationship between husband and wife, which throughout Scripture is used to picture the relationship between God and his people—in the New Testament, specifically between Christ and the church (see, for instance, Ephesians 5:22-33).

We would never want to say that Proverbs' instructions on sexual purity within marriage are symbolic and given only to represent a call for faithfulness to our Lord. But we might say that the more literally and seriously we take Proverbs' instructions in this area, the better prepared we will be to grasp the deep connections between the marriage relationship and that of God with his people. You don't look away from the picture to understand its significance; you look deep into it.

So, let's do that. Having acknowledged the deeper resonances of the issue, let's meet this woman and learn all we can from wisdom's perspective on her.

Instruction 8: First, a Warning and an Urging

The eighth instruction (Proverbs **5:1-23**) brings both warning against the evil path and urging toward the good one, specifically in relation to marriage. The structure is clear:

- Initial call (**v 1-2**)

- Warning against disaster of adultery (**v 3-14**)

- Urging toward joy of marital intimacy (**v 15-19**)

- Final argument against adultery (**v 20-23**)

Let's make three observations about the forbidden woman who stands out in the first half of this instruction. First, we are asked to notice her words. This should not surprise us, as the emphasis on words has been front and central from the book's beginning. The instruction begins with a call we recognize by now: the call to the son to be attentive, to incline his ear to this teaching. But the prospect of the son's *lips* guarding knowledge (**v 2**) is followed immediately by the forbidden woman's *lips* dripping honey: "her speech is smoother than oil" (**v 3**). There is a battle of words here. The son stands in danger of being lured away from wisdom's true words by the woman's enticing ones. The oil and the dripping honey create a sensual allure, but that allure comes not (as we might expect) through the woman's appearance but rather through her words! Proverbs is a book that teaches the life-and-death power of words.

> Proverbs teaches the life-and-death power of words.

Second, the forbidden woman is associated with ruin and ultimately death. She herself has clearly not listened to wisdom, and anyone who listens to her will find her not satisfying but instead "bitter as wormwood" (a pungent, potentially poisonous herb) and "sharp as a two-edged sword" (a weapon sharpened to kill) (**v 4**). Whereas the word of God is sharper than a two-edged sword in the sense of being deeply convicting, in order to bring repentance and life (Hebrews 4:12), this smooth-talking woman is a two-edged sword that brings only death. To follow her is to follow one whose "feet go down to death, / her steps follow the path to Sheol" (Proverbs **5:5**). The final description of her is desperately sad: in contrast with wisdom's counsel to "ponder the path of your feet" (4:26), this woman "does not ponder the path of life; / her ways wander, and she does not know it" (**5:6**). She's a lost soul, and one that leads others to lose their way.

Third, the results of following this woman are not only individual but also *communal*. **Verses 7-14** describe the relinquishing of this man's strength, honor, and profit to a house that is not his. At the end of his life we see not only his personal regret—"How I hated discipline"; "I did not listen to the voice of my teachers" (**v 12-13**)—we see also his communal shame, vividly expressed in his final words: "I am at the brink of utter ruin / in the assembled congregation" (**v 14**). That picture warns us sharply and hauntingly; not only are we threatened with ruin, but as part of God's people we suffer ruin in the midst of the "congregation," or the assembled family of believers. Ultimately our shame is before the Lord and in his house—his family.

Powerful as is this negative warning, even more powerful is the teacher's positive urging toward the opposite of adultery: joyful marital intimacy. Contrasting with the cloying images of oil and bitter herbs, this instruction's second half flows with the imagery of "water" (**v 15a**); "flowing water" (**v 15b**); "springs" and "streams of water" (**v 16**); and a "fountain" (**v 18a**)—all images that celebrate the joys of sexual pleasure within marriage. The water is "from your own cistern … from your own well" (**v 15**). The imagery and the tone are reminiscent of the Song of Solomon, and the message is the same: a celebration of love expressed sexually within marriage. The call is clear: to "rejoice in the wife of your youth" (**v 18b**).

We should wholeheartedly revel in passages like this one, which play a part in pushing back the darkness of sexual perversion that we find around us in our world today. What is wonderful is that the force pushing back the darkness is not rules or duty—although those can be helpful—but rather the goodness of marital love which lights up the landscape and shows up perversion for the perversion it is. This passage unabashedly calls a husband to let his wife's breasts fill him with delight and to "be intoxicated always in her love" (**v 19**). That word "intoxicated" can also be translated "led astray" (as in **v 23**)—but here it's not *led astray*; it's *led home*. And it's good. What's bad, then, stands out by direct contrast in the next lines:

"Why should you be intoxicated, my son, with a forbidden woman
   and embrace the bosom of an adulteress?" (**v 20**)

The instruction concludes by stepping back and showing the big picture, with the Lord God always watching and judging a man's steps. Ultimately it is the *Lord's* "pondering" of our paths that matters (**v 21**); when we follow wisdom's counsel to ponder our path (4:26), we're trying to see as God sees.

The conclusion does not show the Lord stepping in to execute judgment on the man who is led astray. Rather, the picture is of the man being ensnared, bound by his sin, and dying because of his lack of discipline: "Because of his great folly he is led astray" (**v 23**). Ultimately, this is God's judgment, for God created the world to work a certain way. Wisdom is to listen and to follow that way, walking in the fear of the Lord. We've seen here a powerful example of folly, which despises wisdom and instruction (see 1:7) and which leads to death rather than life.

Wisdom Warnings

The final line of chapter 5 reminded us that we're looking down folly's path at this point in Proverbs. We've had an instruction on the folly of adultery, and now, before we have another one, we come to a wisdom section that develops parallel kinds of folly—three of them. Each one ends with the same deadly ensnarement that we saw overtake the adulterer. And all of them by contrast point toward the way of wisdom as the better way.

Chapter 6 does begin with "My son"; you could legitimately argue that this is another instruction. And yet **6:1-19** holds together as a clump of more general warnings, before **verse 20** brings back the typical call of the father to the son to listen to his words, etc. What stands out in this section are the consistent, vivid descriptions of disaster that will suddenly come on those who practice folly.

First comes a warning against putting up financial security for another person (**v 1-5**). We will see this theme again in Proverbs; whenever it comes, it always seems to me to be a little random, and almost a little mean. Why not help another person secure a loan by risking a little of your own money? This seems like an almost ridiculous kind of folly to juxtapose with the terrible folly of adultery that we just encountered. Perhaps that is part of the point: folly has various flavors and different levels. Perhaps the lack of prudence that would put one's own goods at risk is not a different kind but only a different level of the imprudence that would share the intimate pleasures of marriage with strangers.

All kinds of qualifications must bear on this subject: it matters whom we're helping and why, what their situation is, and what ours is; this is not a call not to be generous, but rather to be prudent, and so forth. But the voice of wisdom doesn't take time to add qualifications here; the warning is urgent, and the man must not sleep until he tries to undo a foolish pledge. The final lines give two quick, violent pictures of impending disaster:

"Save yourself like a gazelle from the hand of the hunter,
   like a bird from the hand of the fowler." (**v 5**)

Second comes a warning against laziness (**v 11**). The man who was just told to give his eyes no sleep and his eyelids no slumber until he undid his foolish pledge perhaps needs a bit of nudging; perhaps he's related to the lazy **sluggard** in this section who loves his sleep but who is given a violent wake-up call.

This is the famous call to "go to the ant, O sluggard" (**v 6**); he's asked to consider the industrious ways of the ants and to learn wisdom from them. Without even a ruler to direct her, the ant works to prepare and gather her food, in summertime and at harvest. The ant knows the created order and lives according to it. In a crazy and delightful contrast with the orderly little ant, the big lazy sluggard (who has a ruler and a law) just lies there thinking, "A little sleep, a little slumber, a little folding of the hands to rest" (we all know that feeling!)—until this warning breaks in, again with two quick, violent pictures of impending disaster:

"Poverty will come upon you like a robber,
   and want like an armed man." (**v 11**)

Third comes a warning against one whom we might call the malicious deceiver (**v 12-15**). This man is like the sluggard in that he is "worthless," accomplishing no good (**v 12**). But unlike the sluggard he is active, busily deceiving others, "devis[ing] evil," and "sowing discord" (**v 14**). **Verse 13** shows his whole body alive with his evil: eye winking, feet signaling, finger pointing—like a jerky little marionette villain calling attention to himself on a stage of marionettes. The warning for this fool breaks in quickly, with a more general but just as ominous picture of impending disaster. This figure will collapse:

"Therefore calamity will come upon him suddenly;

in a moment he will be broken beyond healing." (**v 15**)

The section concludes with another zooming out of the lens to see the big picture of what the Lord sees. **Verses 16-19** offer one of Proverbs' numerical sayings, with six and then seven items; such a list often builds to a climax, but it also might suggest that we could go on adding to the list! These things that the Lord hates reach out in all directions in the text, especially to the malicious man just described. The "lying tongue" (**v 17a**) corresponds to that previous figure's "crooked speech" (**v 12b**). "A heart that devises wicked plans" (**v 18a**) corresponds to his devising evil (**v 14a**). "Sows discord" (**v 19b**) corresponds to the almost-identical two words in **verse 14b**; this final evil shows the relationship-breaking result of all the others.

The point is that the Lord sees and hates these evil outpourings of a "perverted heart" (**v 14a**). Folly is not just actions that can be defined as evil. Folly is a personal rejecting of wisdom, which begins with the fear of the Lord. Folly first destroys our relationship with our Creator. Outside of that relationship, all kinds of fools stumble along the path of deep darkness; we've been peering down that path. We've met all kinds of folly, with the folly of adultery highlighted—as it is now highlighted again.

Instruction 9: Back to Adultery

After all the intense warnings, our ears ought to be open to the extended opening call in **verses 20-24**. As in the very first instruction, both father and mother are mentioned as the teachers, perhaps emphasizing the picture of a marriage union that must not be broken. Their teachings are spoken of in terms that often in Scripture refer to the word of God: the son is to bind these words on his heart, and they will lead him and commune with him:

"For the commandment is a lamp and the teaching a light,

and the reproofs of discipline are the way of life…" (**v 23**)

In just the same way the psalmist cries: "Your word is a lamp to my feet / and a light to my path" (Psalm 119:105).

Again in this instruction the evil woman whom we met before emerges; the opening call finishes by claiming that these teachings will preserve the son "from the smooth tongue of the adulteress" (Proverbs **6:24**). As another battle of words emerges, we are meant to understand that the smooth-tongued words of the adulteress are in direct competition with the very word of God.

The instruction develops in two main parts: first, the warning not to be captivated by the adulteress (**v 25-29**); second, the results of committing adultery with her (**v 30-35**). The arguments seem almost surprisingly pragmatic; **verse 32** encapsulates the central point:

"He who commits adultery lacks sense,

he who does it destroys himself."

We must remember that in the world created and ruled by the Lord God, it truly doesn't make sense to rebel against his laws—on any level. And it truly makes sense that the consequences for the deep, deep disorder of adultery would be dire.

Again, note the centrality of marriage and sexual sin related to it. **Verse 26** claims rather enigmatically that the price of a prostitute is only a loaf of bread, but a married woman, by contrast, "hunts down a precious life." This does not mean that prostitution is not grievously wrong; it does mean that the breaking of a marriage through adultery somehow involves an even deeper pain and consequence.

God set up marriage in the very beginning in order to tell us human beings something about himself… something that grows clearer and clearer through the whole biblical story… something about the relationship he has with his people, and will have forever, through the salvation accomplished by Christ Jesus his Son. Marriage is at the heart of God's creation of us, and of God's communication with us. In God's world, adultery truly does not make sense.

We are not yet done with the adulteress. She will make one more dramatic appearance in chapter 7, in the final instruction. We'll actually get to hear those smooth-tongued words and watch her in action. But other voices will speak before we've finished this first section of Proverbs. We must get the final view of the two paths, of wisdom and of folly—and we must hear and respond to the voice of wisdom, calling us to life as opposed to death.

Questions for reflection

1. It has been said that today one version of visiting the forbidden woman is accessing a pornographic website. What parallels do you see?

2. For what reasons is it important for all of us (whether we are married or not) to hear the emphasis on the purity and the beauty of marriage?

3. On another subject (sort of), what do you learn from the ants?

4. WOMEN CALLING

Proverbs' opening section ends as it has progressed: with voices calling. We'll first look at chapters 7 – 8, which offer quite a contrast. In chapter 7 (the final instruction), the father puts a seductive adulteress before our eyes and ears. But then in chapter 8 comes Wisdom calling, with a climactic invitation to hear and follow. Finally, chapter 9 concludes the section with a vivid dramatization of the choice to be made, and the key to making it.

A Story With a Lesson

After the previous two instructions highlighting adultery, the father changes his approach, in this final instruction. There is the familiar opening call for "my son" to listen (**7:1-5**). But what follows is a little narrative: a story the father uses to bring to life the point he's been making. He's a good storyteller. First he artfully establishes the setting (**v 6-9**). Then conflict appears and the tension rises dramatically (**v 10-20**). The climax hits suddenly (**v 21-23**). Finally, the conclusion broadens and drives home the story's point (**v 24-27**).

The opening call urges the son again to keep (used three times) his words. The point is to treasure the words (**v 1**); to find life and delight in them (**v 2**); and not just to hold them with fingers but to write them "on the tablet of your heart" (**v 3**). We're getting to know wisdom by now; we're ready to appreciate the urging to call wisdom "sister" and insight "intimate friend" (**v 4**). We have seen the emphasis on *relationship* from the beginning—and it's this close relationship with wisdom, through her words, that will "keep" the son from the "adulteress with her smooth words" (**v 5**).

The setting is one of the best parts of this masterful mini-drama. The father describes himself looking out from the window of his house, with the vivid detail of looking through the lattice, so that as the story unfolds we never forget we're seeing and hearing it through the lens of the wise father, and in his voice (even when he quotes the woman). This story is his final instruction, meant to be remembered and passed on as such.

He sees this *simple youth* (**v 7**; mentioned in 1:4 as the first audience for this book) who lacks sense (**7:7**, the very description of the adulterer in 6:32), walking near the adulteress's corner, and then on the road to her house (**7:8**; see 5:8). The cross-references in the previous sentence help us see this story as the culmination of all the father's advice about adultery! This setting is quickly drawn, but it pulls together what has come before and sets up the tension for what is to come.

As it grows, the conflict involves four verses of description (**7:10-13**) and seven verses of the woman's words (**v 14-20**). She's dressed like a prostitute (**v 10**) but is a wife (**v 19**)—a wife whose "feet do not stay at home" (**v 11**). "Loud" and "bold," she seizes him, and kisses him… and *speaks* to him. Her speech is indeed "seductive" (**v 21**), appealing to all his senses. Many commentators suggest that her mention of having offered sacrifices implies she has brought home some freshly prepared meat; they can share a meal together. With her words she draws him in—almost to taste the meat, to see her beautifully colored Egyptian linens, to smell the scent of her bed perfumed with **myrrh**, **aloe**, and cinnamon… These are powerful, evocative words. And the young man has not a word to say.

The woman's call is openly deceptive. She admits to appreciating her religious rituals for their tasty leftovers. She urges that they delight themselves with love (recall 5:19), but she openly speaks of her husband, who is away for a long while (**7:19-20**). She is "wily of heart" (v 10) in her perverted desires, but she does not hide from the youth what she's after. In all the portrayals of the adulteress in Proverbs, she is what she is. The point is not to call to her to be different—although that is worthy material for another book and another story. Proverbs' point is that evil temptation is there, and we readers are asked to identify with the one called to resist it.

In this story the youth does not resist. The climax comes "all at once"; we recognize that one little moment of giving in that brings earth-shattering consequences. The text hits us with three quickly drawn, powerful images of animals caught and violently killed:

> One little moment of giving in can bring earth-shattering consequences.

"All at once he follows her,
as an ox goes to the slaughter,
or as a stag is caught fast
till an arrow pierces its liver;
as a bird rushes into a snare;
he does not know that it will cost him his life." (**v 22-23**)

And so we come to the end point: following wisdom's path is a matter of life and death. We can almost hear the father's voice trembling as he closes, so desirous is he that his son—and all sons (**v 24**)—listen to his words and keep their hearts from turning to this path of folly that we've witnessed. Again the lens widens, and the father pictures "a mighty throng" of those slain along this woman's path (**v 26**): "Her house," says the father, "is the way to Sheol, / going down to the chambers of death" (**v 27**).

How shall we process this lesson today? The world around us would deride such counsel about avoiding adultery; the very concept of adultery assumes certain foundational truths about marriage that many dispute. We can't help but notice, however, that many of the fiercest public battles involve issues of gender and sexuality—and marriage. As we've said, these issues involve the heart of our humanness. From a biblical perspective, they involve our creation as human beings in the image of God, male and female—ultimately together serving and worshiping him as his body, his church, redeemed by his Son.

Proverbs' wisdom lands hard on these issues in its introduction, asking us to look deep into the temptation of adultery and to prize deeply the good of marital faithfulness. This one path of wisdom versus folly is the same path of wisdom versus folly that we all experience every day, in a multitude of ways, from how we lend money to how well we work to how we treat the people around us. A heart full of wisdom's words makes the difference between being drawn aside to folly or kept on the path that leads to life—in a relationship founded on the fear of the Lord.

That's where we're headed next, as Proverbs' first section draws to a close. We're headed toward the sound of Wisdom's voice, taking in her words, which make all the difference.

Wisdom Calling

Moving from the voice of the adulteress in chapter 7 to the voice of Wisdom in chapter 8 is an exhilarating leap. These are both portraits of women calling out for people to listen and follow. Whereas we saw the adulteress leading many down to death, however, we now see Wisdom offering life to many. The adulteress speaking in chapter 7 was a real, in-the-flesh woman: in fact a woman ensnared in sensual and fleshly pleasures. In chapter 8, on the other hand, Wisdom is a reappearance of the personified figure we have seen before, most clearly back in 1:20-33, where she was crying aloud and raising her voice in the public places of the town.

In the introduction to this fourth and climactic wisdom section, we find Wisdom again calling and raising her voice in public places where people of all kinds are likely and able to hear (**8:1-3**). The wonderful truth, as the beginning and end of this speech remind us, is that these words keep mercifully calling us even now, sinful and simple as we human beings are.

The speech in chapter 8 falls into three main sections between the introduction (**v 1-3**) and the concluding call (**v 32-36**). First, Wisdom speaks about the nature of her *words* (**v 4-11**). Second, she speaks of the *benefits* she brings (**v 12-21**). Third, she speaks of her *identity* (**v 22-31**). In these sections, Wisdom is revealing herself more and more clearly; it's as if she is lifting her veil, and we can only marvel at what we get to see.

Her Words

Wisdom's call to hear and follow her words (**v 4-11**) sounds a lot like the father's many calls to hear his words. Surely we are meant to make that connection: these personal voices in Proverbs are both offering the same wisdom, grounded in the fear of the Lord. There is no other wisdom. There is only one source: the Lord. Wisdom's speech here has that truth at the heart of it.

Wisdom cries out to "the children of man" (**v 4**); this call is for everyone. The next verses identify the "simple" and the "fools"; they are the ones that stand out—and everybody stands out like that at some point, needing to be steered along the straight path by the voice of wisdom. Wisdom's words can be trusted, for she will speak "noble things" and "what is right"; she will "utter truth," words that are "righteous" and "straight" (**v 6-9**). We're reminded of the "crooked speech" that we've been warned about (4:24; 6:12) and that we've heard coming from another woman's mouth (**7:14-20**). Wisdom explicitly notes that "there is nothing twisted or crooked" in her words (**8:8**).

The comparison with silver, gold, and jewels (**v 10-11**) will sound familiar: Wisdom is here singing the hymn from chapter 3, echoing its claim that wisdom's gain is better than silver or gold (3:14) and that wisdom "is more precious than jewels" (3:15). There, we were told that "nothing you desire can compare with her"; now, it's "all that you may desire cannot compare with her" (**8:11**). The point is this: *Listen! My words will tell you truth—truth more valuable than anything else you could ever seek.*

Her Benefits

After claiming this kind of value for her words, Wisdom goes on to explain this value, naming some of the benefits she brings (**v 12-21**). Again we find a mini-cluster of those weighty wisdom words that were introduced in the prologue: "prudence," "knowledge," "discretion," "wisdom," and "insight" (**v 12-14**). And again the stated foundation is "the fear of the LORD" (**v 13a**)—which, consistent with the book's message, makes a dividing line between wisdom and folly. That fear, says Wisdom, "is hatred of evil"; she reiterates that she *hates* pride, arrogance, and perverted speech (**v 13**).

Verses 15-16 apply her benefits specifically to political leaders, emphasizing the just rule that wisdom enables kings, rulers, princes, and nobles to exercise. Certainly these "proverbs of Solomon, son of David, king of Israel" (1:1) are the fruit of this truth, shining in the context of the people called out by the Lord God to be his own. But "all who govern justly" (**8:16**)—including any wise earthly ruler—have been granted wisdom by the Lord who is the source of it.

Wisdom gives a worldwide call here; she would give her benefits near and far. We've heard her address "the children of man." And now she is calling people with one qualification: that they love her. "I love those who love me," she says, "and those who seek me diligently find me" (**8:17**). We should stop and meditate on this verse. It contains reverberations of God's words to his people, for example in Deuteronomy 4:29: "You will seek the LORD your God and you will find him, if you search after him with all your heart and with all your soul." In the Scriptures we hear the voice of God calling his people—ultimately his people from all the nations—and promising that when we answer his call and seek him, by his grace, he will be found by us (Jeremiah 29:13-14). More than that, he loves us. These benefits are personal.

Proverbs **8:18-21** overflows with the treasures of love: riches and honor, wealth and righteousness—an interesting combination of physical and spiritual gifts, but all better than gold, even fine gold (**v 19**). This is the "inheritance," says Wisdom, given "to those who love me" (**v 21**). An inheritance outlasts death; there is a clear sense here of lasting treasure, even eternal treasure, waiting for those who seek after wisdom with all their hearts.

Her Identity

In **verses 22-31**, the speech rises to its most exalted point. Wisdom here reveals her identity as one who has been with God from before creation: "The LORD possessed me at the beginning of his work" (**v 22**). The Job-like poetry asks us to imagine eternity past:

"When there were no depths I was brought forth,

when there were no springs abounding with water.

Before the mountains had been shaped,

before the hills, I was brought forth." (**v 24-25**)

"Possessed" in **verse 22** has stimulated much discussion, which we cannot adequately cover here. The sense of this word, however, seems most clearly to be not that Wisdom was created by God at some point (as some earlier translations suggested), but rather that Wisdom is generated by God—similar to "brought forth" in **verses 24-25**.

The thrust of this section moves to Wisdom's presence with God in creation: "When he established the heavens, I was there" (**v 27**). The Lord asked **Job**: "Where were you when I laid the foundation of the earth?" (Job 38:4). Wisdom is saying that she was there—and not only that. Here is the most amazing claim, referring to the time of creation, when the Lord assigned to the sea its limit and marked out the foundations of the earth:

"Then I was beside him, like a master workman,

and I was daily his delight,

rejoicing before him always,

rejoicing in his inhabited world

and delighting in the children of man." (Proverbs **8:30-31**)

These words resonate with truths that unfold later in redemption's story. Consider, for example, the opening verses of the Gospel of

John: "In the beginning was the **Word**, and the Word was with God, and the Word was God. He was in the beginning with God. All things were made through him" (John 1:1-3).

What John writes about the Word, Wisdom in Proverbs claims about herself. As the master workman at God's side, Wisdom is presenting herself as God's agent of creation, the one through whom all things were made. Wisdom is claiming the role that the New Testament attributes to God's Son—the Word that was made flesh and dwelt among us (John 1:14). Paul says that "all things were created through him and for him" (Colossians 1:16).

These echoing connections should fill us with wonder at God's eternal plan as it is unfolded, all pointing ultimately to Jesus. But we should keep in mind the context of Proverbs, which comes at a specific point in this unfolding. We've seen that this figure of Wisdom is not presented as any kind of divine appearance, but rather as a picture (a personification) that points toward something greater. In light of all of Scripture, we can say that this picture, while not being Christ, points ahead toward Christ. Kidner writes, "The personifying of wisdom, far from overshooting the literal truth, was a preparation for its full statement" (*Proverbs: An Introduction and Commentary*, page 79).

Once God's full statement of his Word is given in Christ, then we get to hear the New Testament writers fully celebrating that Word as "Christ Jesus, who became to us wisdom from God" (1 Corinthians 1:30)—and "Christ, in whom are hidden all the treasures of wisdom and knowledge" (Colossians 2:2-3). Proverbs points ahead to this fullness, picturing it truly through its God-breathed words.

In the midst of these theological discussions, we mustn't miss the overflowing joy and delight of this passage. Note how "delight" and "rejoicing" weave a pattern of joy in the goodness of God's creation in Proverbs **8:30-31**. The delight lands on the same audience that Wisdom addresses: the children of man (**v 4b**; **v 31b**). Wisdom's call in Proverbs is not an abstract call to virtue; it is the Lord's call to the human beings he created in his image, for his glory—and joy!

Wisdom's conclusion (**v 32-36**) addresses "sons," plural, echoing the father's voice and offering a final comprehensive call. The invitation is to "hear instruction and be wise," and the promise is blessing (**v 32, 34**; see also 3:13) for those who will watch at Wisdom's gates and wait beside her doors. The final two verses give concluding clarity to the two paths: "Whoever finds me finds life," says Wisdom; and "all who hate me love death" (**8:35-36**).

Questions for reflection

1. The story of the young man (Proverbs 7) is a vivid story of being tempted and giving in. What parts of that story ring true in your own experience?

2. Pick a couple verses from chapter 8 just to read aloud and enjoy. What do those verses reveal about God?

3. Jump to the end of the Scriptures, just for a moment, and read Revelation 5:11-12. How is wisdom finally on full display in that scene?

PART TWO

This Woman and That Woman

If chapter 8 is the high point of the book's first section, chapter 9 is the perfect landing point, and the perfect preparation for the next section to come. With all these voices calling, it's clear that we must respond. That's what the final chapter of this section asks us to do.

First, an overview of this chapter's structure will be helpful. A beginning section and an end section are balanced against each other; more specifically, two women are directly competing against each other: Wisdom (**9:1-6**) and Folly (**v 13-18**).

Many commentators see these two female figures as contrasting personifications: female figures that picture the qualities they represent. For Wisdom, this is not problematic; we have seen this personification before. For Folly, this is slightly more complicated; not only have we not met this personification before, but we have heard about some women in the flesh who sound a lot like her. It will be easy to recognize the adulteress in this portrait.

You could make the case that this one *is* that one—that Folly in chapter 9 is a real woman, the adulteress. You can make a better case, I think, that this one is different—that Folly in chapter 9 is, like Wisdom, a personification, picturing for us what folly is all about. Yes, Folly is pictured like the adulteress, but here she is not called the adulteress; she is called Folly. And what is highlighted are not the details of her adultery, as we will see; rather, what stands out is that this woman offers the opposite of what Wisdom offers: ultimately, death versus life.

We'll look into the details of the portraits. At this point let's see two directly contrasting figures at either end of the chapter—with wise instruction in between (**v 7-12**). Some see these verses as a continuation of Wisdom's quoted words. That is certainly possible. However, the direct and dramatic contrast between **verses 1-6** and **verses 13-18**

makes it more probable that these sections stand parallel to one another in this chapter, and that the mid-section stands distinct.

That middle section connects thematically in both directions, to
Wisdom and to Folly. But the most important reason to see the central
section as central is that right in its center comes the main point of the
chapter—and, indeed, a reprise of the main point of the whole book,
as we will see.

Wisdom Up Close

Before getting to the center, let's examine the chapter's opening and
closing sections. We start where the chapter starts: with Wisdom.

We've seen the personification of wisdom before, but not at home.
She has previously been out in the busy areas of the town, calling for
all to listen to her words. But now she's been at work at home, and it's
her young women she sends out to do the calling "from the highest
places in the town" (**v 3**).

Before the calling comes the setting (**v 1-3**). We should stop to relish the details. Every short statement in this description has Wisdom
as its subject: this is all about what she has done—and she has done
it all:

"Wisdom has built her house;
  she has hewn her seven pillars.
 She has slaughtered her beasts; she has mixed her wine;
  she has also set her table." (**v 1-2**)

The scene is obviously Wisdom's house, where she has prepared a
great feast. She started seriously from scratch: she built the house
to begin with. The seven pillars are much discussed, but many end
up saying these pillars probably show just how big and grand this
house is, with room for many. In the Scriptures the number seven
often symbolizes perfection or completeness (see, for instance, Revelation 1:12-20); these pillars could well point to those qualities in
Wisdom and her work. The point is that Wisdom has done the work,

from down-and-dirty labor to perfect finishing touches. What a progression: from hewing down great pillars, to slaughtering beasts for meat, to mixing the wine, to setting the table. She has done it all for her guests; all they have to do is come in and feast with her.

After the setting comes the call:

"Whoever is simple, let him turn in here!"
  To him who lacks sense she says,
"Come, eat of my bread
  and drink of the wine I have mixed.
Leave your simple ways, and live,
  and walk in the way of insight." (Proverbs **9:4-6**)

Notice first the audience for her call: "whoever is simple" and the one who "lacks sense." What was the first audience mentioned in the book's prologue (and numerous times after)? It was "the simple" (1:4)—the immature one, often the "youth." Who was the victim of the adulteress in chapter 7? A simple youth, "lacking sense" (7:7; see also 6:32). This chapter's final picture operates in the context of the first nine chapters, speaking to every human being, yes, and focusing especially on the one who has not yet found the good path—or who is tempted to wander from it.

That special focus emerges in the nature of this call, which asks the simple person to change direction: "Turn in here" (**9:4**) and "Leave your simple ways, and live" (**v 6**). Those two phrases take her call from the details of the physical picture right to the meaning of the picture. The text itself makes clear that we are reading a symbolic portrayal of the call to turn from death to life, through words of life that show the way.

Biblical Resonances

We must take care in developing the meaning of these pictures. It is important to observe context and avoid **allegorical** leaps that pin down one-to-one correspondences of this to that. The meal in Wisdom's house is not an Old Testament picture of the **Last Supper**. However, in our care, perhaps sometimes we don't allow ourselves to enjoy the whole-biblical resonances in Old Testament and New. The word "resonances" helps, implying that we can hear echoes and understand how themes connect and grow throughout the Scriptures, without forcing them into charts and lists of specific symbolic meaning.

Feasting in the presence of the Lord, for example, is a biblical theme that stretches enticingly throughout the Scriptures. There is that mysterious scene in Exodus 24, when Moses and seventy of the **elders** go up on the mountain and glimpse the shining glory of God's presence. Moses sums up what they did there: "They beheld God, and ate and drank" (Exodus 24:11). And the theme of feasting in God's presence grows and grows. Think of God's institution of all the feast days as part of the Israelites' regular ceremonial worship. There was the Feast of Unleavened Bread, which was associated with the Feast of Passover; the bread and meat consumed during those feasts commemorated God's rescue of his people from their slavery in Egypt. Those feasts were all about what God had done for his people.

Later, the prophets spoke of future feasting in God's presence. Isaiah, for example, pictured a scene that resonates closely with Wisdom's feast:

"On this mountain the LORD of hosts will make for all peoples
    a feast of rich food, a feast of well-aged wine,
    of rich food full of marrow, of aged wine well refined."

                                   (Isaiah 25:6)

Resonances increase as the redemptive story unfolds. The promised Lamb of God, God's own Son, comes to save his people, and he not only multiplies loaves and feeds crowds of thousands, but he says to his disciples, "I am the bread of life" (John 6:35). And he explains what he will do for them so that they can eat and drink and live: he will lay down his life (John 6:50-55). He will do all the work of salvation on their behalf, so that they can live.

The book of Revelation ties together this theme of feasting with more pictures, again letting us peer into realities that we cannot yet fully understand. As the **Bride of Christ**, we believers look forward to that marriage supper of the Lamb, when we will be clothed in "fine linen, bright and pure" (Revelation 19:6-9). Here's a symbol that is explicitly explained: we're told in Revelation 19:8 that "the fine linen is the righteous deeds of the **saints**." We're also told that "it was granted [the Bride] to clothe herself" in this linen. It was granted to us to be righteous, because someone else did the work for us, on our behalf. Jesus died in our place and rose again. Trusting in him, we get to go in to the feast.

> Not until Jesus comes again will we understand exactly how these themes all come together—but the Scriptures are full of hints.

Wisdom has done the work and invites us into her house, to feast on the bread and wine she has prepared for us.

I've taken the time to explore a few of these resonances because they are so beautiful and rich. Of course, the best way to enjoy them is not to look up a word and find all the references, but rather to be always reading through our Bibles and watching these sorts of themes take on meaning, as the Bible unfolds. Not until we get to the end of the story ourselves, when Jesus comes again, will we understand exactly how these themes all come together, in him. But the Scriptures are full of hints: hints that feed our souls in the meantime.

Folly Up Close

The woman Folly has surprising similarities to Wisdom, and yet deadly differences. Her section begins not just with the setting but with a narrative comment on her character: "She is seductive and knows nothing" (Proverbs **9:13**). That word "seductive" takes us back to the honey-dripping words and "seductive speech" of the adulteress

(5:3; 7:21). That she "knows nothing" tells us this is the extreme example of lacking sense.

Folly has no creativity to make anything herself; she can only imitate. Several of the phrases in Folly's section mimic Wisdom's section word for word. Folly also stations herself "on the highest places of the town" (**9:14**). The first part of her call is identical (compare **v 16** and **v 4**). She is also promising food and drink.

But the similarities cannot cover up the differences. Interestingly—in contrast to Wisdom who works so hard—Folly is sitting down by her door. She offers not wine she has mixed herself, but stolen water (**v 17**), which recalls by contrast the refreshing water drunk "from your own cistern" (5:15). Wisdom would turn the simple from their simple ways; Folly is calling to those passers-by "going straight on their way" (**9:15**), aiming to turn them to hers.

The final two verses expose the folly of the pleasure she offers, as they reiterate (again!) the life-and-death truth of what is at stake here (see 2:18-19; 5:5; 7:27):

"But he does not know that the dead are there,
> that her guests are in the depths of Sheol." (**9:18**)

The truth repeatedly taught is, of course, not that if you commit adultery you will immediately die (though that was actually the punishment taught in the Old Testament law—see Deuteronomy 22:13-30—and "Sheol" is literally the place of the dead, not hell, but simply the grave.) But we gather here that folly's path brings death on many levels, with no eternal hope held out. The path of the righteous, we've seen, is a path that grows ever brighter until the full light of day (4:18). The path of the wicked is a path of "deep darkness" (4:19), as far ahead as we can see.

The Key at the Center

How shall we tell the difference, then? How shall we teach the next generation, the youths around us, to go into the house that is full of life and feasting, not the one that leads to death?

The key, as stated, is at the chapter's center:

"The fear of the LORD is the beginning of wisdom,
   and the knowledge of the Holy One is insight." (**9:10**)

This verse not only holds the chapter together, by giving the key to choosing wisdom over folly; it also forms an "inclusio" (a kind of sandwich) with the same key statement of the prologue in verse 7 of chapter 1. These two verses are bookends that hold the whole first section of the book together.

Only in a relationship with the Lord, fearing him and listening humbly to his words, can anyone discern the right house. Watching and waiting at Wisdom's doors (8:34) lets us know her and learn to recognize her voice—and the voice of any imposter. Only this personal "knowledge of the Holy One" gives the insight we need. The Lord through his word here is calling us to know and follow him, and only him.

As we follow him, fearing him, we are enabled to receive wise words wisely—which we will need to do when we reach chapter 10. That's what chapter 9's middle section emphasizes: **9:7-9** contrasts the ways in which a wise and a foolish person receive instruction. In sum, the fool hates and abuses the teacher; the wise man loves the teacher and learns wisdom.

Verses 11-12 point ahead to the result: in **verse 11**, it's more and more life for the one who is listening to wisdom. **Verse 12** offers a sober warning that each person will experience the result individually. We cannot hide in a crowd along with the wise or the foolish. Knowledge of the Holy One is personal knowledge. How amazing that this grand divine wisdom reaches each of us personally, through God's word, and ultimately through the Word made flesh, who came and dwelt among us.

We are now warned and prepared to receive the instruction to come in the individual proverbs. The warnings have been sober, but the promises of life along wisdom's path are overflowing with blessing.

Questions for reflection

1. How do you experience every day the conflicting voices of wisdom and folly calling?

2. We found the fear of the Lord at the center of chapter 9, and bookending chapters 1 – 9. Stop and sum up some of what you are learning about the fear of the Lord in Proverbs.

3. In what ways does the figure of Wisdom show you the blessings of salvation in Christ?

5. READY FOR THE PROVERBS?

The book's opening section (chapters 1 – 9) has helped us understand the beginning of wisdom as the fear of the Lord. On that foundation we are prepared to receive the instruction of the "proverbs proper," beginning in chapter 10. First we'll talk about what these proverbs are, and how the poetry works. Then we'll dig into chapter 10, giving attention to specific proverbs.

What Is a Proverb?

We haven't discussed it much so far, but we've been reading poetry all along in Proverbs. Wisdom literature can include both poetry and prose (think of Ecclesiastes), but the book of Proverbs is all poetry, of a variety of kinds.

First, what is poetry? As opposed to prose, which develops ideas through what we usually see as paragraphs, poetry is more concise language, usually appearing on our pages in lines. Poetry is carefully patterned, condensed language; it says the most in the fewest words. And it often uses pictures, or imagery (as we've seen), to communicate.

In much of Proverbs' first nine chapters, we find poetry that develops ideas over a number of lines. But in chapter 10 we meet the collection of proverbs. Some of them cluster and form larger units of meaning, but many stand alone as individual proverbs. So, what is a proverb? People often say a proverb is like wisdom in a nutshell: it's *especially* condensed poetry. A proverb is a short and pithy saying, easy to remember.

According to the scholar Leland Ryken, a proverb brings a "moment of epiphany": that is, a quick highpoint of insight (*Words of Delight*, page 315). It often just makes you say "Yes!" as you suddenly see some truth with intense clarity. "A joyful heart is good medicine, / but a crushed spirit dries up the bones" (17:22). Yes! "Like a gold ring or an ornament of gold / is a wise reprover to a listening ear" (25:12). Yes!

We should note that individual proverbs are found not just in Proverbs and the wisdom books; they appear throughout the Bible. Jesus sometimes used this way of teaching, as we noted in the **Sermon on the Mount**. The **epistle** of James is full of proverbial sayings: for instance, "The one who doubts is like a wave of the sea that is driven and tossed by the wind" (James 1:6). But the book of Proverbs is a remarkable concentration of these concentrated sayings.

Parallelism: Rhyming Thoughts

Let's focus on two main characteristics of Proverbs' poetry: parallelism and imagery. These two elements characterize all Old Testament poetry, but their effect is condensed and heightened in the individual proverbs.

First, parallelism—which refers to the balancing together of parallel units of meaning. When we're reading proverbs in translation from the original Hebrew language, we usually see the parallel units of meaning as distinct poetic lines—most often two lines at a time ("couplets"). In this book I am referring to the units of meaning as "parallel lines," even though in more technical discussions we'll find terms like "colon" (one unit of meaning); "bi-colon" (two units of meaning balanced together, or a couplet); "tri-colon" (three units of meaning together). Whatever the terminology, the point is to notice the parallelism of ideas. Hebrew poetry has many distinct technical features, but it depends for its essential meaning on parallelism. The poetry is given to us, as I've heard some teachers say, not mainly through the rhyme of sounds but through the rhyme of *thoughts*.

As the father's opening instruction began, in Proverbs 1:8, the scene was quickly set with a proverbial couplet:

> "Hear, my son, your father's instruction,
>> and forsake not your mother's teaching."

> Hebrew poetry is given to us not mainly through the rhyme of sounds but through the rhyme of *thoughts.*

The corresponding parts are easily discernible: "hear" and "forsake not"; "your father's" and "your mother's"; "instruction" and "teaching." We noted earlier the way these lines capture both the positive call to hear and the negative warning not to forsake. We celebrated the familial fullness of father and mother together passing on wisdom. All communicated in two little parallel lines!

The marvel is that God in his providence set up his word to work this way. Most poetry cannot be translated very well at all; you just can't capture elements like rhyme and **meter** in translation. But Hebrew poetry does not depend primarily on those elements for its meaning; what it depends on can actually be captured quite well in translation.

The ideal scenario is that you and I would become experts in Hebrew, so that we could spend our time reading these texts in the original language. But, for now, let's stop to wonder and delight ourselves in the fact that we can read a good translation and get the true essence of the meaning God intended. Here's how C.S. Lewis puts it:

> "It is, according to one's point of view, either a wonderful piece of luck or a wise provision of God's, that poetry which was to be turned into all languages should have as its chief formal

characteristic one that does not disappear (as mere metre does) in translation." (*Reflections on the Psalms*, pages 2-3)

I recently spent several weeks teaching in France. What a joy to gather with our open Bibles, whether in English or in French, and to let the word of God penetrate our hearts! My husband and I have friends who are translating the Bible into the language of a remote tribe in Papua, Indonesia. How amazing to visit and to see Papuan pastors, teachers, and school children holding copies of Scripture translated into their own language, and to know that the word of God is meant to speak with clarity into every human heart, no matter our language or culture.

Parallelism in Action

As we read, we'll notice the parallel lines balancing together in a variety of ways. I'll summarize three widely accepted categories of parallelism, admitting that these categories greatly simplify what is a complex and often uncategorizable flow of ideas. However, if we learn to use these categories in a careful and nuanced way, they can be extremely helpful.

First, sometimes the two parallel lines say almost the same thing: that's often called *synonymous parallelism*. The lines are never exactly the same; part of the point is to watch for the differences as well as the similarities. Consider 22:24:

"Make no friendship with a man given to anger,
    nor go with a wrathful man…"

The two lines give basically the same advice—and yet there is a revealing progression. In the first line it's a man "given to anger," suggesting someone who tends to get angry a lot. In the second line it's a "wrathful man"—using a stronger, more violent word for anger to define him. The change from "making friends" to "going with" may suggest the progression of a relationship that uncovers just what kind of person this is. So, here is a warning about what not to do, along with some thought-provoking hints about what might happen if you do it. In fact, as we'll see when we get to that section, the subsequent verse unfolds exactly what might happen.

Synonymous parallelism often pushes the meaning deeper, or makes it more vivid, in the second line. Consider the familiar proverb:

"Pride goes before destruction,
and a haughty spirit before a fall." (16:18)

The two parallel lines refer to the same truth—yet the second line is more concrete. The first line states the big principle; the second makes us think about how that principle is experienced by haughty-minded people who, just when they are thinking highly of themselves, suffer some sort of humiliation that puts them in their place. Maybe we have experienced that kind of fall ourselves. Or maybe we're in danger of it. (Or maybe there's even another way to think about the relationship of these lines together.)

Second, sometimes the two parallel lines say opposite sorts of things: that's often called *antithetic parallelism*. Again, the lines are never exactly opposite, so part of the point is to watch for the surprises. Proverbs is full of antithetic parallelism, which should not surprise us in this wisdom literature that so clearly shows the two opposite paths of wisdom and folly.

Proverbs 15:1, for example, points out the contrasting effects of wise versus foolish words on an angry person. But there are surprises in this simple proverb, which plays with the same parallel between "anger" and "wrath" that we noted before. Here, the point seems to be not just that a soft answer and a harsh word bring opposite results; the soft answer (ironically) is even more powerful, able to turn away the more violent evil:

"A soft answer turns away wrath,
but a harsh word stirs up anger."

The third category can be called *synthetic parallelism*. This category often works as a "catch-all" bin for various other kinds of parallelisms. Sometimes the parallel line just completes a thought:

"Do not boast about tomorrow, / for you do not know what a day may bring" (27:1). Often the proverb simply draws a comparison: "Like a gold ring in a pig's snout / is a beautiful woman without discretion" (11:22).

Many different categories and sub-categories of parallelism have been suggested. This is not an exact science. Sometimes a proverb does not fit a category, or it could fit several. The point is not to get categories right. The point is to grasp the nature of this parallelism, which puts ideas in relationship with one another, as one unit of meaning interacts with the parallel unit in order to communicate. As we learn the way this poetry works, we receive more clearly the meaning intended by the poet—and ultimately by the God who breathed out these magnificent words.

Imagery

Speaking of gold rings in pig's snouts, let's turn to the second main characteristic of Proverbs' poetry. Along with parallelism, what stands out in this poetry is the imagery—the picture-language.

It's the pictures that make many of these pairs of lines so pithy and worth pondering. The *imagery* makes us stop and *imagine*—and we must take time to do that, instead of rushing to get the lesson being taught and moving on to the next. Stopping to ponder the pictures actually protects us from the danger of moralism; we can't just jump to the moral if we're taking time to process the pictures.

This poetry seeps into our minds and hearts as we chew on it, so to speak. Some like to talk about sucking on the proverbs like hard candy: if you bite down fast, you just break your teeth; but if you suck on it slowly, the flavor emerges.

So, are you picturing that pig's snout? Have you seen a real pig's snout, especially after the pig has been rooting around in its slop or in the mud? I've been reading the children's book *Charlotte's Web* with my grandchildren, and it's certain that the writer of Proverbs did not have in mind anything like E.B. White's delightful pig named Wilbur. The picture of Proverbs 11:22 is disgusting, ridiculous, awful; and so we consider how it reveals the truth about a beautiful woman without discretion—how worthless and wasted her physical beauty is if she lacks wisdom's good judgement and self-control. She's like a gold ring in a pig's snout.

I quoted earlier 25:12: "Like a gold ring or an ornament of gold / is a wise reprover to a listening ear." Here's a gold ring in the right place, shining. We have already noted the imagery of gold, silver, and jewels associated with wisdom and shining from the book's first nine chapters (for example, 1:9; 2:4; 3:14-15; 8:11). An alluring chain of precious gems and metals and graceful adornments stretches through Proverbs' text, lighting up our imaginations and our desire to grasp the beauty and the value of godly wisdom.

We've already seen remarkably vivid pictures, ones that awaken our senses—several violent hunting scenes; street scenes with women crying out; paths lighted and paths in deep darkness; scenes of eating and drinking; dripping honey; bitter herbs; sharp swords; refreshing fountains; lovely deer; ants gathering food—and we'll see many more. They will fly by on the pages, but I hope you will take time to stop and ponder them.

Parallelism and imagery are the poetic engines of this poetry. They are not just extra decoration for the ideas. God did not inspire just the ideas behind the words; he inspired the words themselves, which were written exactly as God intended, by writers who were carried along by the Holy Spirit (2 Peter 1:21). We should take care with everything about these words, including the poetic form. This is one part of waiting by Wisdom's door.

Questions for reflection

1. How often do you read poetry? Why do you think God breathed out so much of it in his word?

2. In what ways does the culture around you fill your mind with images, coloring your imagination? How might the images in God's word help "sanctify" our imaginations?

3. What are some pictures Jesus used to reveal himself and his truth to us? Why are they so effective?

PART TWO

The Swirling Themes of the Proverbs

The "proverbs proper" begin with the largest collection, called "The proverbs of Solomon" (10:1 – 22:16). Chapter 10 immediately immerses us in a variety of themes that seem to swirl all around us. Actually, we noted the same cycling repetition in the first nine chapters, but there the themes were channeled through distinct instructions and wisdom sections. That was like swimming in a bay with lots of strong currents; now, with chapter 10, we're out in the open ocean, often feeling tossed around from one theme to another, and back and forth.

Perhaps you have seen lists of themes addressed by Proverbs, as many books and studies organize themselves around those themes. That can be a helpful approach, as we gather into separate categories all the proverbs relating to work, money, words, marriage and sex, and so forth. (We might think to ourselves that if we had edited Proverbs we might have done a better job of helping readers process these themes.) We feel more organized with a clear thematic approach, which lets us contemplate wisdom's complete teaching on one subject after another.

What we should ask first, here, is why God gave us the proverbs in this swirl. Biblical wisdom literature is not unique in its collections of proverbs; other ancient cultures created and passed on such collections as well, with similarities in format—and whatever true wisdom was included in the wisdom literature of other cultures was the gift of God's common grace to human beings all made in his image. But, as we've said, Proverbs is unique wisdom literature, breathed out by God the divine author, written and edited by Solomon and a few others, all under God's sovereign hand. And so our question is a good one: why did God give us the proverbs in this swirling form?

We've already seen the kaleidoscopic nature of wisdom, starting in the prologue, and we've watched Wisdom calling out all over the town. Wisdom in Proverbs invades every big and little part of life.

Perhaps here is the starting point for the answer to the swirl: Proverbs' wisdom invades every part of life, and the book actually shows us that real-life process.

We human beings don't wake up in the morning and deal first with our marriage and family issues, and then our money issues, and then our tongue, all in a logically planned order. No—from the moment we wake, life actually comes at us in the same kind of fluid chaos that Proverbs presents as it teaches us that wisdom is applying God's truth to all of it, all of life, in all its messiness. How wonderful that God sees and speaks into what so often feels like the chaos of our lives. This truth has to make us think of Jesus, who actually came into the messiness of human life, with blood and sweat and joy and pain on all sides, to redeem all of it—every part of it.

> Wisdom is applying God's truth to all of life, in all its messiness.

A friend once commented to me that if the themes were organized into categories, we would probably just pick the categories that we think we need, or that we want to focus on. Another pointed out that this amazing swirl of proverbs makes vivid the process of searching described in the book's first section: aiming to understand the "riddles" of wise words (1:6) and searching for wisdom as for hidden treasures (2:4).

The Basic Contrast Is Clear

Amid the swirl, certain themes and even clusters of themes emerge distinctly. As Proverbs 10 leads us into the collection of proverbs, the first five verses make clear the basic thematic contrast at work: it is the fundamental contrast introduced in chapters 1 – 9, that of wisdom and folly. Antithetic parallelism dominates this part of the proverbs, making the contrast vivid.

After all the calls to "my son" in previous chapters, **10:1** is a delightful and satisfying transition, with its opening words: "A wise son…" But we must read the whole couplet, which immediately sets up the contrast:

"A wise son makes a glad father,

   but a foolish son is a sorrow to his mother."

I'm not sure exactly why the mother gets the sorrowful line. It is true, however, and happily true, that mother and father together here share the involvement with their son; the couple is joined by the couplet! 1:8 and 6:20 showed them both teaching him; 4:3 showed generations of parents together; here, now, we have father and mother experiencing the joy and the sorrow of sons who follow either wisdom or folly.

The proverbs express this fundamental contrast in terms of righteousness and wickedness—the qualities we have seen along the paths of wisdom and folly, respectively. (Recall 4:10-19, for example, where the father's instruction pointed toward the path of the righteous and away from the path of the wicked.) The "righteous," then, are the people walking wisdom's path, in the fear of the Lord. This doesn't mean they're perfect. In fact, often the point is that they listen to rebuke, and they repent and change. The "wicked," by contrast, walk folly's path: not listening, and heading toward death rather than life.

In the full light of Scripture, we know that only one man has ever lived a completely righteous life: Jesus Christ, the Son of God. He received God's full rewards, and believers receive those rewards in him. The "righteous" in Old Testament times looked ahead in faith to this righteous One who would come to save, offering himself as the perfect sacrifice for the sins for all who believe (Romans 3:21-22; 4:3). The ceremonial sacrifices only pointed to that final sacrifice. But in following God's word, Old Testament believers put their faith in God's provision for their sin; we do the same, in the full light of the gospel. The "wicked" did not and do not heed God's word; they follow their own path.

The next two verses (Proverbs **10:2-3**) continue to trace this basic contrast between righteous and wicked, both showing the better outcome of righteousness. **Verse 2** makes an intriguing comparison:

"Treasures gained by wickedness do not profit,
but righteousness delivers from death."

In cases of antithetic parallelism, as we look for the surprises, it's help-ful to ask what we might expect the second line to say if it were ex-actly opposite to the first. We might expect, then, in line 2, to read *But treasures gained by righteousness do profit*. Instead, the treasures are not even there. Perhaps the word is simply understood, as sometimes happens in second lines where a parallel word is not stated but im-plied. In any case, all we have in line 2 is righteousness; it is righteous-ness itself that is the great treasure and that does not just bring some temporary profit; it actually delivers from death.

Verse 3 offers a similar reward for some chewing. What might we expect as the opposite of "The Lord does not let the righteous go hungry"? We find not just that he lets the wicked go hungry, but that he actively "thwarts" not merely the hunger but the "craving" of the wicked. This proverb reveals so much: God's care for those who follow him; God's punishment of those rebelling against him; and also the nature of those who rebel.

Verses 4-5 continue the fundamental contrast, turning it toward the subject of work, contrasting wisdom's diligence and prudence with folly's slackness and laziness. The rewards are riches and poverty, respectively. **Verse 5** returns to the figure of the son, who seems to hold these five verses together. We sense the gladness that a father (or mother) would have in this prudent son (**v 5a**), but the sorrow that a mother (or father) would have in this lazy "son who brings shame" (**v 5b**). We also have a larger context for the literal riches and poverty, having just been reminded of the greatest profit of righteousness: de-liverance from death (**v 2**). We'll return to this subject of rewards.

Time and space will not allow detailed discussion of every proverb. Our method from here will therefore be to move through chunks of proverbs as they come in the text, often focusing on themes and con-nections within those chunks—but inevitably leaving some individual proverbs less covered. My prayer is that what we cover more carefully will pave the way for further and productive study on your part (and on mine).

The Theme of Words in Proverbs 10

Proverbs **10:6** begins a scattered but discernible cluster of proverbs in this chapter, relating to words and the tongue. "The mouth of the wicked" holds the cluster together, in **verse 6** and **verse 32**. We've already met this theme, and we'll meet it again. There are some themes that we don't encounter immediately when we get up in the morning—but the theme of words is not one of them. So here it is, right away!

Chapter 10's proverbs on words continue the contrast between the righteous and the wicked:

"Blessings are on the head of the righteous,
 but the mouth of the wicked conceals violence." (**v 6**)

Why is the righteous person who receives blessings on his head contrasted with the wicked person whose mouth conceals violence? Perhaps the wicked person's hidden evil cuts him off from receiving blessing. In the case of the righteous person, we see his head and can imagine someone speaking words of blessing even while placing a hand of blessing on his head (as fathers did in blessing their sons; see, for example Genesis 48:14-18). In the case of the wicked person, we see only his mouth; it's taken over the picture.

This wicked person is evidently talking, but his speech is like a deceptive cover. Violent thoughts and intents lurk behind his words. The same picture is repeated in Proverbs **10:11**, with a more direct contrast:

"The mouth of the righteous is a fountain of life,
 but the mouth of the wicked conceals violence."

The wicked person hides evil behind his words; by contrast, the righteous person sends forth good through his words: we picture a fountain flowing forth without concealment, giving pure, life-giving water.

More contrasts emerge and connect in this passage. Picture that beautifully shaped, life-giving fountain we just saw. Then, by contrast, picture water bubbling uncontrolled: that's what the wicked person's words are like. Even though the wicked person is described three times as "concealing" evil behind his words (**v 6b, 11b, 18a**), his words still bubble forth. He's a "babbling fool" (**v 8b, 10b**). The prudent person "restrains" his lips, but for the evil person "words are many" and "transgression is not lacking" (**v 19**).

What is inside a person is the key. Hidden inside the evil person, behind his babbling words, is violence—evil intent. But inside the righteous person we find something very different. Here is a deep contrast:

"The wise of heart will receive commandments,

but a babbling fool will come to ruin." (**v 8**)

Inside the wise person is a heart open to wisdom, to wise words—ultimately to the commandments of God's law. There's nothing concealed; rather, there is openness to receive, and consequently fullness to pour forth blessing like a fountain of life. What comes out is beautiful: "The tongue of the righteous is choice silver" (**v 20**). But that verse's second, contrasting line makes this awful judgment, returning to what's inside: "The heart of the wicked is of little worth."

Applying Wisdom's Words on Words

How do we apply these words on words practically? There's no doubt that these words are applicable to all human beings. We are created as word-creatures in the image of our word-speaking God, who spoke and created the world; who mercifully speaks to us in his breathed-out word; who finally sent us the Word made flesh, his own Son.

But oh, how we show our fallenness and our sin through our words! How quick we are to speak, to "babble," and in fact to hold onto evil thoughts or intents behind our words. These are truths not much considered by our culture. Few around us are telling us to restrain our words; on the contrary, we are encouraged on all sides to speak and write all that we think and feel and do—in fact, to post the words so that hundreds or thousands can read them. Yet we all recognize that our words are somehow out of control. They so often don't bring refreshment or life to others; often, they hurt.

Here is the point at which the proverbs can be either misused or used well. The tendency, when applying proverbs, is for me to clench my jaw and try to do what they say (or to hope that person I'm think-ing of will get the point and do what the proverbs say). When I read proverbs about restraining the tongue, I might resolve to control my words better than I have done. I'll go off social media for a while. I won't lose control when I'm talking to that irritating friend or family member and say things I will regret.

And of course I will fail. I will fail if I try to apply the moral like a whip, either to myself or others.

The key is there for us in Proverbs. Wisdom kept calling to us about it. It's fearing the Lord, living in relationship with him, reverencing him for who he is, and humbly listening to his words of life. The key is here in this passage as well: it is having the kind of heart, first of all, that receives God's word. Our words are just the outflow. Jesus said, "Out of the abundance of the heart the mouth speaks" (Matthew 12:34). He promised to give water that will become in us a spring of water welling up to eternal life (John 4:13-14).

How would Proverbs send us off to work on our words? Proverbs would call us in to open our hearts to God's word—which will trans-form our hearts, and as a result, our words. And it will happen through Jesus the Word made flesh, who came and dwelt among us, who died to save us, and whose Spirit lives in us who believe.

Final Contrasts

Let's note one other theme introduced in chapter 10: that of future rewards.

Proverbs is well known for associating good rewards with good behavior, and bad outcomes with bad behavior. Many refer to it as

Proverbs' "character-consequence" connection. The first thing to say about this is that it is often true. According to the way the Creator God set up his world, for example, laziness often does cause poverty, and diligent work usually brings good results—as we saw in Proverbs **10:4**. Think of agriculture: if you don't till the soil and pluck the weeds and work hard at harvest time, then you'll probably reap a poor harvest—and vice versa (**v 5**).

But the second thing to say about this association is that it is not *always* true. The proverbs are not rules or promises. They give insight into the order of God's creation: an order that those who fear him will want to know and respect. But that order has been disrupted by sin. That's why, along with the many proverbs connecting good rewards with good behavior, come the ones acknowledging that sometimes it's the other way round—the opposite is true. Before **10:4** comes **10:2**, where we see that sometimes treasures are gained by wickedness. We need to read *all* the proverbs.

And we need to watch for the layers of time implied in the rewards. The timing is often not clear. Many of the rewards are material and **immanent**; but many reach out to an undefined progression of time. Proverbs does not define eternal states, but it often stretches our thoughts ahead, sometimes into eternity.

For example, in chapter 10, numerous times it is stated that the man of deceitful and babbling words will come to "ruin" (**v 8b, 10b, 14b**). We feel the ruin coming, even as the violence inside him builds up and threatens to blow up—but we don't know when. The following two proverbs look ahead to good and bad results that stretch out in the future, even to "forever":

"What the wicked dreads will come upon him,
    but the desire of the righteous will be granted.
When the tempest passes, the wicked is no more,
    but the righteous is established forever." (**v 24-25**)

We read all these individual proverbs in light of the first nine chapters and their teaching about wisdom, and folly, and life, and death—

and the fear of the Lord. There will be regular reminders of the foundation that has been established. **Verse 27** stands out:

"The fear of the LORD prolongs life,

but the years of the wicked will be short."

From the midst of the proverbs shines the foundational light: the fear of the Lord that is the beginning of wisdom—wisdom that brings life as opposed to death. Rich life now is in the foreground. But never out of sight is the prospect of life forever with the Lord we fear.

A final comment: in every chapter, some proverbs seem to pop up alone. **Verse 26** about the sluggard is one of them. We've met the sluggard already; he was getting a little sleep (6:6-11). We'll meet him again. He's one of those irritating figures who keep showing up as we're carrying on our business. We'll deal with him later; he'll still be there.

Questions for reflection

1. Old Testament believers were called "righteous" as they trusted in the Lord and his promises. How do "righteous" believers today receive those promises which are now fully revealed (see 2 Corinthians 5:21; 1 Peter 3:18)?

2. Can you remember a time when you said something you wish you had not said? What was going on in your heart?

3. Pick one proverb from Proverbs 10 that you'd like to "chew" on. Why that one?

6. THIS WAY AND THAT WAY

We're out in the open sea of proverbs, surrounded by the "proverbs of Solomon" that began in chapter 10. Chapter 11 sets forth a clear God-centered perspective and continued contrasts between the righteous and the wicked; we'll give specific attention to the theme of wealth. In chapters 12 – 13 the contrasts continue with increasing vividness, and with a renewed, lively focus on words and their various effects.

Remember the LORD

We saw the fear of the Lord shining its light in the midst of chapter 10 (10:27). Periodically, in Proverbs, a mention of the Lord lights up the text and makes sure we haven't forgotten the foundation of wisdom. The proverbs really do reflect the flow of real life, in which we believers in fact do not talk about God all the time. But we talk about him regularly, hopefully often, acknowledging the reality of his constant holy presence and his merciful revelation through his word. Proverbs' periodic mentions of the Lord are like that: not random but regular, and carefully planted throughout the book, as we'll see more and more clearly.

Proverbs 11 mentions the Lord twice, both times enlarging our perspective: from looking up to fear or to receive blessing, to momentarily seeing human life through the Lord's eyes. The first instance gives a sense that he is peering into our every business deal:

"A false balance is an abomination to the LORD,
	but a just weight is his delight." (**v 1**)

This verse not only lights up God's perspective on dishonest business dealings (a "false balance" would be a rigged scale that weighs or measures unfairly for our profit), but it also opens up the context of God's revealed law, of which the Israelites would have been well aware. Leviticus deals clearly with such matters. I quote this passage with a bit of context—all of which would have been ringing in the Israelites' ears:

> "You shall do no wrong in judgment, in measures of length or weight or quantity. You shall have just balances, just weights, a just **ephah**, and a just **hin**: I am the LORD your God, who brought you out of the land of Egypt. And you shall observe all my statutes and all my rules, and do them: I am the LORD."
>
> (Leviticus 19:35-37)

As is true throughout the law, the point is not rote obedience. The point is that the one speaking is the Lord—the God who mercifully redeemed his people from slavery and who then reveals to them just how to live in relationship with him.

> These issues are not abstract; they are a matter of eternal weight.

The connection between Proverbs 1 – 9 and the rest of the book is not unique, but affirmed throughout Scripture. First comes the relationship with the redeeming Lord, whom we fear; then, listening to his word, we learn to live in that relationship. The New Testament epistles fully illumine this connection by means of the gospel: first we come to Christ, believing the truths of who he is and what he has done to accomplish our redemption, and then, as new creatures in Christ, we learn how to live in him, according to his word.

The aspect of relationship is highlighted in Proverbs **11:1** by language expressing God's powerful response: he finds either "abomination" or "delight." These words suggest strong emotions, helping us grasp how personal is the Lord's response to these seemingly abstract legal issues. These issues are not abstract; they are a matter of eternal weight, of offending or delighting the Lord himself.

One proverb like this helps light up the whole sky above all the proverbs. And there is a string of such lights. Consider the chapter's second mention of the Lord:

"Those of crooked heart are an abomination to the Lord,
　but those of blameless ways are his delight." (**v 20**)

The same words, "abomination" and "delight," reveal the Lord's response, but here it is as if the Lord peers even deeper in, into the very hearts of the cheaters. And those hearts are "crooked." We've seen this word "crooked" in reference to unrighteous words (4:24; 6:12; 8:8), and we've seen the picture of the straight path of righteousness (4:25). In **11:3**, the integrity of the upright is contrasted with the crookedness of the treacherous. Clearly, "those of crooked heart" have rejected the fear of the Lord; they are an abomination in his eyes.

We often forget to imagine what our daily doings look like to our Lord God. We worship him on Sunday and then so easily forget him as we turn to the work that fills our week. Do we hear heaven's reverberations on Monday when we fudge a number on a report, for our own benefit? If a store clerk fails to charge us for one of our items, and we notice but don't call attention to the omission, does this seem hardly worth a thought, or are we attuned to the personal response of our all-seeing Lord?

Wealth and Warnings

The string of lights illuminating the array of proverbs helps us process Proverbs' repeated contrasting rewards, which are connected not just to human behavior but ultimately to the Lord God, who judges all human behavior. The rest of chapter 11 continues the contrasts, continuing as well the antithetic parallelism that dominates this first part of "The Proverbs of Solomon."

The theme of wealth and riches emerges often in Proverbs 11. Interestingly, in the midst of Proverbs' numerous promises of material blessing for the righteous, many of this chapter's proverbs give another perspective. We've noted that these sayings are not rigid rules, but true observations revealing the pattern of order established by the Creator God. As creation is fallen, these observations will include instances of disorder as well—discernible as disorder of course only in light of a foundational sense of order.

Back in chapter 10, we sensed the ambiguity concerning riches: yes, diligence brings riches (10:4b), and the Lord's blessing "makes rich" (10:22a)—and yet treasures can be "gained by wickedness" (10:2a). The sense of warning grows even stronger in chapter 11. Violent men get riches (**11:16b**), and "the wicked earns deceptive wages" (**v 18a**). Consider two proverbs that appear early on in the chapter:

"Riches do not profit in the **day of wrath**,
　　but righteousness delivers from death." (**v 4**)

"When the wicked dies, his hope will perish,
　　and the expectation of wealth perishes too." (**v 7**)

Both of these proverbs deal with the futility of riches in light of death. In **verse 4**, the "day of wrath" is not defined; it points ahead with ambiguous timing toward some disaster, torment, or judgment in which riches, ironically, will bring no "profit." The contrasting parallel line looks to righteousness for deliverance from death; this parallelism associates the day of wrath with death, and makes clear that that day, whenever it comes, will not bring death to the righteous.

Such proverbs can easily be misused, and often are. A person could read this out of context and conclude that if we live a righteous life then, when we get cancer, we will not die, but be healed. Or, if the "day of wrath" turns our thoughts ahead to God's judgment (which in light of the whole of Scripture, or of **verse 1** and **verse 20**, it might), we may conclude we need to live a righteous life in order to avoid the divine wrath to come. Without setting "righteousness" in the context of the whole book, grounded in the fear of the Lord, we can end up depending on our own righteousness to appease God and earn his favor.

In the end, trusting in riches and trusting in our own righteousness have a lot in common. They both reject wisdom from above. **Verse 7** reinforces the futility of such trust, not just in this life but after death. Every once in a while, in this section of predominantly antithetic parallelism, a different sort of parallelism pops up. That happens here, with the verse's second line not making a contrast but adding a further, related truth. The change in poetic rhythm makes us stop and notice this emphatic point that gets two pushes in the same direction.

We might expect "hope" and "expectation of wealth" to be in reverse order, as the perishing of hope might seem more finally and completely devastating. But we're told first that in death (here implying physical death) the wicked person's hope perishes—and then that his expectation of wealth perishes as well. *So,* asks the proverb, *had you thought your wealth might still be able to help you, when all other hope is gone? No,* says Proverbs. *There's no hope there, in anything you've earned.*

Riches for the Righteous

On the other hand, all kinds of riches are associated with the righteous. We've seen Proverbs' character-consequence connection. Generosity brings riches (**v 24**). The one who blesses others will be "enriched" (**v 25**). In **verse 18** we noted the wicked person's "deceptive wages," but the parallel line reads, "One who sows righteousness gets a sure reward." Well, what kind of a reward? The parallel with "wages" may imply a similar monetary treasure, but this time one well earned.

It's also possible that the "deceptive" nature of the wicked person's wages (physical, but with no lasting security) points by contrast to the secure or lasting value of a spiritual "sure reward." More light comes from the very next proverb, which addresses the rewards of righteousness and evil:

"Whoever is steadfast in righteousness will live,

but he who pursues evil will die." (**v 19**)

So, what do "life" and "death" mean? We're not given a timeline. Proverbs' own picture of the path helps here—this picture that was established repeatedly in chapters 1 – 9 and recurs regularly thereafter (see, for example, 10:17; **11:5**; 12:28). Although Proverbs does not stop to define specific timelines, it always pushes ahead toward the future—along a path of either life or death. One is the path of wisdom, filled with those who fear the Lord and listen to his word. The other is the path of folly, filled with those who despise wisdom and instruction.

After **11:19** comes the Lord's perspective on the two ways in **verse 20**, which we have seen already. Then **verse 21** sets us back down along the way, looking ahead to see the punishment that will come to the evil person (who rejects the fear of the Lord) and the deliverance that will come to the offspring of the righteous (who fear the Lord). We don't know when these will come. It seems that punishments and deliverances mark the pathway all along. But our gaze is drawn ahead—far ahead.

It's the pictures of the life enjoyed by the righteous that draw us. We have in our minds the picture of the path that grows ever brighter until full daylight (4:18). Along this way we're seeing fountains of life (10:11) and treasures of choice silver (10:20). We also find green leaves and trees—life in nature picturing human life that flourishes in relationship with the Lord:

"Whoever trusts in his riches will fall,

but the righteous will flourish like a green leaf." (**11:28**)

"The fruit of the righteous is a tree of life,

and whoever captures souls is wise." (**v 30**)

There was a glimpse of this tree early on in the book: wisdom "is a tree of life to those who lay hold of her" (3:18). We look back to that tree in the Garden of Eden, giving "life forever" to the one who eats of it (Genesis 2:9; 3:22). We look forward and glimpse that tree in the heavenly Jerusalem, growing alongside the river of the water of life, yielding its fruit each month, forever (Revelation 22:1-2). Pictures of rich, never-ending fruit fill our minds.

The rich life associated with the righteous is the rich life of wisdom, lived in relationship with the Lord. And it's a life that grows. Those pictures in Proverbs 11, in **verse 28** and **verse 30**, show righteous people themselves as flourishing and green, bearing the fruit of wisdom. **Verse 30** is one of those non-antithetic parallelisms that stops the section's normal flow and rings with special emphasis: in this case an emphasis on the spread of life. "Capturing souls" in this context looks like drawing others into wisdom's life. In the context of the completed Scriptures, it looks like leading people to Jesus, who is the way, the truth, and the life (John 14:6).

Spreading Effects of Wisdom and Folly

In Proverbs **11:9-14**, a cluster of proverbs highlights the communal effects of wisdom and folly lived out—with a focus again on the tongue. Many of the proverbs we've looked at so far emphasize individual lives and results; these verses reach wider.

They reach out first to a person's "neighbor"—the one we interact with in daily life. Three proverbs (**v 9, 12, 13**) describe how a fool (a "godless man," "lacking sense") brings harm to his neighbor simply through his words: "belittling" him, or "slandering" him by revealing secrets or suggesting untruths. The wise person (one with "knowledge," "understanding," a "trustworthy spirit") by contrast holds his tongue.

Who could not tell a story of being harmed in some way by another's belittling or slandering words? And who could not describe a desperate desire to take back some words that hurt a person near us?

I once heard a man at a party making fun of his friend standing next to him—all seemingly good-natured. The issue was the friend's loud snoring, which this man described in rather crude detail, to the amusement of the men and women listening. The laughter soon, however, became rather embarrassed, as people realized that the "snorer" was looking very uncomfortable with these private details being so mockingly exposed. He was a shy person, and in fact that evening his companion was a woman he was coming to care for deeply. That's a small example. But even those silly words caused some mortification. Think of the harm of disclosing deep griefs, perhaps speaking of them lightly, or exposing mistakes from years past that a person has painfully worked through. Think of thought-less comments that make fun of a friend's parents or family mem-bers. Think of the deadly harm of planting wrongful accusations in people's minds. A trustworthy person uses discretion to protect his neighbor.

Verses 10-11 put before us not one neighbor but a whole city. Both lines of **verse 10** insist on rejoicing; the contrast comes between the prospering of the righteous and the perishing of the wicked. That is a satisfying contrast, with both lines showing justice—and bringing "rejoicing" and "shouts of gladness" from a city.

Verse 11 returns to a more normal contrast, and a vivid one: the basic claim is that through the words of the righteous or the wicked, a whole city can be either exalted or overthrown. Today's news head-lines would offer up examples of both, although it might be easier to locate the poisonous political rhetoric that gurgles like water through the gutters than to find the carefully chosen words of guidance spo-ken with restraint by a wise leader (of a city or of a nation).

We haven't touched every verse of chapter 11. More digging will be required. But we finish by seeing the couple of fleeting glimpses of women in this chapter. After all the mention of women in chap-ters 1 – 9, we might feel their absence here in the proverbs proper. But they pop into view now and again, noticeably. **11:16** sets up an unusual contrast: one gracious woman who gets honor, and a bunch of violent men who get riches. The woman clearly wins, in both char-acter and consequence.

This verse is not a statement about women in general: we mustn't forget the beautiful but indiscreet woman in **verse 22**. These two women may set up a kind of opposition in this section, offering yet another example of the contrasting ways of wisdom and folly.

Questions for reflection

1. How might we be tempted to blur the distinction between righteousness and wickedness that Proverbs makes so clear? Can you think of an example?

2. How do the verses on wealth in these chapters relate to Jesus' words in Matthew 6:19-21?

3. What are some specific ways in which other people's words have brought blessing and life to you?

PART TWO

Establishing Order

Chapters 12 and 13, which we'll look at together, continue to build up the pattern of ordered contrasts that dominate the first part of this collection. It is worthwhile to stop and note the effect of taking in this flow. As we read, we begin to expect the contrasts, and the character-consequence connections. We begin to feel the established, trustworthy order of the universe—in fact, the order set up by the Lord who rules it.

As we come to large, sweeping contrasts like the following ones, we can begin to understand better, in context, how these truths describe God's sovereign patterns rather than giving promises to be applied to any and every particular situation:

"No one is established by wickedness,
  but the root of the righteous will never be moved." (**12:3**)

"The wicked are overthrown and are no more,
  but the house of the righteous will stand." (**v 7**)

These two proverbs, with their pictures of unmoveable roots and stable houses, ask us to grasp the sense of solid, ordained order for the righteous. Those who defy God's order will encounter the logical opposite: no roots, no lasting house—they are destroyed.

Several proverbs in these chapters play ironically with this sense of order, showing the futility of trying to reverse it. "Better to be lowly and have a servant," says **verse 9**, "than to play the great man and lack bread." In other words, it's better humbly to accept one's low position (with, actually, a servant to help you) than to pretend to be a big shot when you're actually broke. For all sorts of reasons people like to try to reverse the order, but reality keeps asserting itself:

"One pretends to be rich, yet has nothing;
  another pretends to be poor, yet has great wealth." (**13:7**)

The proverbs keep tracing the patterns: the diligent will rule, and the slothful will be laborers (**12:24**). Such claims accrue, one after another, in the text; so wisdom begins to shape our sense of this world that belongs to the God who made it.

Words of Reproof

We must return to the theme of words, because these chapters so consistently take us there! In the past, I've sometimes underestimated the peculiar persistence of this theme; if we make it just one of several that we treat with equal time or space, we will miss the way the book keeps returning to this subject. Proverbs winds the theme of words through its chapters just like words wind their way through the days of our lives. We've heard Proverbs' primary call to hear wisdom's words. This subject of words is at the heart of wisdom.

Proverbs **12:1** introduces a specific aspect of words that is extensively developed through chapters 12 – 13: words as reproof or rebuke, to which a wise person listens (and a foolish person doesn't). The contrast couldn't be stronger than in **12:1**: it's a matter of love versus hate. The one who "loves discipline" (associated with reproof) shows that he loves something even greater: "knowledge" (closely associated with wisdom). In contrast, the one who hates reproof is simply called "stupid."

> Proverbs winds the theme of words through its chapters just like words wind their way through the days of our lives.

My grandchildren are not allowed by their parents to call anybody or anything "stupid." Occasionally I say the word and receive their reproof. This verse, however, does not mean "stupid" in the sense of "incapable of learning" or "ridiculous." Rather, this "stupid" has the same meaning as the phrase we've seen: "lacks sense." It is sensible to reason that one could learn and grow from discipline's reproof, and so to listen. It's stupid not to.

Verse 2 does not at first seem to connect directly with **verse 1**'s idea of reproof—although its mention of either favor or condemnation from the Lord, rewarding good or evil, might lead us to consider the "discipline" and "reproof" in **verse 1** as carrying larger ramifications than we first imagined. This verse again lifts our eyes to the Lord; in the light of that perspective, it's clear that the stupidity of hating reproof is stupidity with eternal consequences.

Some of the related proverbs point us toward God's word as the ultimate instruction that must not be refused. Consider **13:13-14**:

"Whoever despises the word brings destruction on himself,

but he who reveres the commandment will be rewarded.

The teaching of the wise is a fountain of life,

that one may turn away from the snares of death."

In the immediate context, the "word" would be the word of wisdom's instruction. In the whole-book context, the "word" and the "commandment" allude to God's word given to the people of Israel, as mentioned in the book's opening verse. (And in fact the word turns out to include the very words of wisdom we are reading!) Here again, revering or despising the word of wisdom (the word of the Lord) is a matter of life and death.

The word of wisdom is for all of us a word of reproof, indeed given "that one may turn away from the snares of death" (**v 14b**). This word draws attention to the futility of foolish ways, and calls a person to turn from those ways, into the path of life. It makes sense that Wisdom's first call was mainly a call of rebuke: "If you turn at my reproof..." she cried (1:23).

The theme of reproof continues insistently in this section. The one who rejects instruction is variously called a "fool" whose way is right in his own eyes (**12:15a**); a "scoffer" who does not listen to rebuke (**13:1b**); one showing "insolence" and bringing strife (**v 10a**); one who "ignores" instruction and invites poverty and disgrace (**v 18a**).

It is enlightening to read a verse like 2 Timothy 3:16 in relation to this theme. Perhaps sometimes we don't notice the prominence of reproof in that famous verse: "All Scripture is breathed out by God and profitable for teaching, for reproof, for correction, and for training in righteousness." In a fallen world, God's word comes always to sinful people, and so it will keep calling us to turn from our sin and receive his mercy, grace, and righteousness. "Reproof" and "correction" are key components of this call.

Because of our sin, it is not easy for us to receive reproof. We naturally do not want to be told we are wrong; it makes us feel put down. We hold on tight to that sense of "being right in our own eyes" (Proverbs **12:15a**), wanting to justify ourselves. My husband has noted a number of times that I tend to react too quickly to a new idea or a proposal that sounds wrong to me, without hearing fully and thinking through what that idea involves. When he makes this observation, of course my immediate impulse is to object, which rather proves him right! I need that reproof. Especially with those close to us, how crucial it is to cultivate the restraint and respect that enable us to listen well, even when we are hearing reproof.

Words of Truth and Power

Proverbs 12 in particular focuses on the truthfulness of our words. We find a clear distinction between truth and non-truth:

"Whoever speaks the truth gives honest evidence,
but a false witness utters deceit." (**v 17**)

In a day when this distinction is disappearing, we hear all kinds of arguments about the fluid and debatable meanings of words—whether those are the words of a public figure, of a legal document, or of the Bible. Yes, words do have nuances of meaning, and, yes, we receive and interpret words according to our own **interpretive grids**, depending on our personal experience. But, no, says Proverbs, we cannot throw away the **objective** meaning of words. Some words can be judged as "true," and some as "false," depending on whether they are honest (corresponding to "honest evidence") or deceitful (not corresponding to honest evidence).

Words, then, correspond to a greater reality than our own personal experience. The whole Bible affirms this truth, telling us that this word comes from God's mouth (2:6); it comes down to us like the rain and the snow from heaven (Isaiah 55:10-11). The proverbs about truthful words reach out to this larger context:

"Truthful lips endure forever,

but a lying tongue is but for a moment." (Proverbs **12:19**)

The largest context comes with the Lord's perspective, given in relation to this issue of truth and falsehood:

"Lying lips are an abomination to the LORD,

but those who act faithfully are his delight." (**v 22**)

Again we see the same two words, "abomination" and "delight" (see 11:1, 20). Here, the contrast balances lying lips against faithful actions, implying that lying lips involve even more than just false words; they involve our character. The Lord looks down and sees our hearts and all our actions, including our words.

Our natural bent is toward lying. If we ever doubt this, spending time with toddlers cures us. Little people lie. "Did you hit your friend?" we ask the little girl who just hit her friend. "No," comes the answer. "Did you take her pencil?" we ask the little boy who just took the little girl's pencil. "No," comes the answer. The cutest little people in fact hit and steal and lie about it.

And so we older people discipline the little people, all the while teaching them to turn to God for forgiveness and help to live the faithful life that delights him. And by God's grace we grown-ups learn the lessons we are teaching. Paul includes lies as a prominent part of the "old clothes" we are to put off when we come by faith to new life in Christ (Colossians 3:8-9). Among the evildoers that Revelation reveals will be thrown into the lake of fire at the end of human history are "all liars" (Revelation 21:8), including the great deceiver, the devil: a "liar and the father of lies" (Revelation 20:10; John 8:44).

When we speak of true and false words, we're talking about the fundamental spiritual battle of the universe. Satan is a defeated liar;

Jesus the Son of God is the way, the truth, and the life (John 14:6). In him is our only hope. Wisdom's words in Proverbs 8 rightly pointed us toward him:

"For my mouth will utter truth;
wickedness is an abomination to my lips." (Proverbs 8:7)

Next time we are tempted to speak words that are not honest and straight, we can remember that the Lord is looking down; we can remember the grace of the Lord Jesus who came down to free us from our sin, taking our penalty in our place.

Our dilemmas when it comes to deciding whether to speak truth or falsehood are bigger than answering "Did you hit your friend?" or "Did you take her pencil?" But the issue of whether or not our words honestly correspond to reality is the same. What exactly did you promise the new worker joining your organization? What exactly was your part in the project that went wrong? What exactly did you say to that person who is hurt or angry? Or, have you ever said you've completed a job when you're basically almost done—but not really done? Did you say accurately how much you spent on that meal or that coat?

God's people have a distinct understanding of the power of words. God created the world by speaking words. In his image we speak and make things with words, whether ordinary conversations or poems or marriage covenants; we humans are word-creatures like our Maker. Jesus is the Word—the Word made flesh (John 1:1, 14). No wonder Proverbs highlights the life-and-death power of words. Wicked words can "lie in wait for blood," and righteous words can bring deliverance (Proverbs **12:6**). Rash words are like "sword thrusts," but the wise tongue brings healing (**v 18**). A good word is so powerful it can make an anxious person glad (**v 25**).

Contexts

The themes dealt with so far are ones all humans know well: wealth, work, words. These themes develop through the consistent use of large contrasting categories: wisdom versus foolishness and righteousness versus wickedness. And yet there is a grounding in the real world that makes these categories understandable. The context of *concrete, ordinary life* is always there.

Verse 9, for example, did not simply speak of humility and pride; it took us into two households: one with a servant and one with no bread to eat. The subsequent proverb stays at home and tells us that a righteous person "has regard for the life of his beast" (**v 10a**)—a lovely glimpse of a most concrete kind of mercy.

The next proverb pictures concretely the reward of diligent labor: "Whoever works his land will have plenty of bread" (**v 11a**). The context is obviously an agrarian society—a context ripe with examples that are not hard for anyone to picture and grasp. Even if we've never hunted game for our dinner, we understand that "whoever is slothful will not roast his game" (**v 27**).

Another important context is that of *the family*—a context evident from the beginning of Proverbs, with the parents' (and grandparents') wisdom passed on to the son. That context is regularly alluded to. For example, another woman makes her appearance in this section—this time a wife (actually, two wives):

"An excellent wife is the crown of her husband,

   but she who brings shame is like rottenness in his bones."

(**v 4**)

We'll come back to the "excellent wife" when we reach Proverbs 31; but it is important to see these two wives here taking part in the antithetical rhythm. The contrasting results could not be more vivid, specifically for the husbands: a wife is either a crown for her husband or she's rottenness in his bones.

The family context keeps emerging. These are the relationships among which we live out our lives, as generations come and go. Again in **13:1** we're reminded of that wise son who hears his father's instruction. **Verse 22** speaks of the goodness of leaving an inheritance to children's children; and **verse 24** brings up a family-related subject we'll return to: that of not sparing the rod but rather being diligent to discipline a child we love.

The largest context of these chapters is that of *the eternal Lord God who watches over each step along our pathways.* We've seen the proverbs that look up to acknowledge the Lord. We've also seen a few proverbs that break the rhythm of predominantly antithetic parallelism, with special emphasis. One of these concludes chapter 12:

"In the path of righteousness is life,
    and in its pathway there is no death." (**12:28**)

This proverb should capture our attention. The second line does not contrast with but affirms the first, with added emphasis on "life" by specifying "no death." Life wins in both lines. We're looking full ahead, along the path of life.

For all its dire warnings, Proverbs is a book that holds forth the promise of life, if we will listen. When we read again of the "tree of life" (**13:12**) and the "fountain of life" (**v 14**), these pictures light up lasting hope. The largest context of Proverbs is a context of life and hope, found in the Lord himself, as we fear him and follow him.

Questions for reflection

1. Can you think of a time you received reproof from someone? How did it go?

2. How does the world around us tend to regard lies? How and why is Proverbs' perspective different? (See also Colossians 3:1-10.)

3. How might these proverbs so far affect your prayers?

7. THE LORD AT THE CENTER

This section takes us to the midpoint of "The Proverbs of Solomon"—and it turns out to be a significant midpoint indeed. We'll first examine chapters 14 – 15 to see the themes growing there; then we'll see those themes unite and culminate in a central passage: Proverbs 16:1-9. Here at the heart of Solomon's proverbs is reiterated the heart of this book's concern: living in the fear of the Lord.

Two Ways

In Proverbs 14 – 15 three strong themes continue to grow, the first being that of the *two ways*, of wisdom and folly. We've seen this pattern from the start of this collection (10:1): using predominantly antithetic parallelism, the proverbs have consistently observed a direct contrast between the ways of wisdom and folly. That contrast goes by various names ("righteousness" versus "wickedness," for example), but the fundamental difference is the one explained from the book's beginning: the way of wisdom is the way of one who fears the Lord and listens to his word; the way of folly is the way of one who despises the Lord and his instruction. One way leads to life, and the other to death.

Chapter 14 opens with a striking picture of the two ways—striking because it takes us back to chapter 9's picture of the two women calling. "The wisest of women" here in **14:1** reminds us of personified Wisdom in 9:1, who built her house, just as this woman is doing. Wisdom's house in chapter 9 was a place of abundant life, with a feast laid out by Wisdom's own hands; chapter 14's wisest of women evidently gives herself to be a similar sharer of life with those around her. The picture is again of a *house*: a place where you *live*.

The parallel image helps explain: "Folly with her own hands tears it down" (**14:1b**). This contrasting foolish woman (who reminds us of the woman Folly in 9:13) is tearing down no physical house but rather the life-filled connections with the people around her. "With her own hands" graphically lays the responsibility on this woman who breaks relationships; such was the "forbidden woman" of chapters 1 – 9, "who forsakes the companion of her youth / and forgets the covenant of her God" (see 2:16-19). That woman's house was described as sinking down to death; she tore it down with her own hands.

Again, two women picture the two ways, making vivid the alternative paths available to every human being. Certainly to women in particular these pictures speak tellingly, pointing toward the ways in which a woman actually can build up or tear down the stability of the lives around her, creating either a safe, life-giving place or else a place of destruction where the life is sucked out of the people she touches. A woman can tear apart her family—and so of course can a man: see 11:29 and 15:27—verses that show the wicked in various ways "troubling their own households." Surely one concrete piece of evidence of folly's hand in the world around us today is the breakdown of marriage and the family, with many "houses" and "households" full of troubled spouses and children looking for a place to live.

The Two Ways in Action

Proverbs **14:2** explains the two ways one more time: the one walking in uprightness fears the Lord, and the "devious" person despises him. The crux is one's attitude of heart toward the Lord God.

This attitude is manifested in the way one "walks," or lives. We've seen examples of honest dealings versus dishonest ones, truthful words versus lies, and so forth. The examples continue in these chapters, with folly showing more and more of its colors. We've just seen "folly" tearing down her house. In **verse 9**, fools "mock at the guilt offering": the verse implies scorn of the worship instituted by the Lord himself. By contrast, "the upright enjoy acceptance": evidently the Lord accepts that offering, forgiving the "upright" who fear him and follow his word.

In these chapters, we find fools acting and speaking recklessly, without restraint:

"One who is wise is cautious and turns away from evil,
 but a fool is reckless and careless.
A man of quick temper acts foolishly,
 and a man of evil devices is hated." (**v 16-17**)

The blustery fool takes over the stage in those two verses, quickly displacing the contrasting wise, cautious figure. Of course, Proverbs is quick to show the coming turn-around, with another couplet that points to the consequences to come:

"The evil bow down before the good,
 the wicked at the gates of the righteous." (**v 19**)

That foolish temper, though, flares up again and again—an unmistakable marker of folly's path. The understanding person is "slow to anger," but the one with "a hasty temper exalts folly" (**v 29**). Do you know this angry person? Are you this person, sometimes? It's easy to recognize anger in another person, and to realize its harm as we hear harsh words wielded like weapons or witness harsh actions that hurt deeply. It's also especially easy to justify our own anger, not seeing it with others' eyes and feeling only the self-satisfying rush of emotion with which anger feeds us. Angry people are puffed up by the violence of their feelings; it's impossible to be humbly fearing the Lord and giving oneself to unrestrained anger at the same time. These are two different paths.

There is such a thing as righteous anger. But Proverbs is dealing with the anger most of us know much better: unrighteous anger coming from an impure heart. Many of us will have witnessed a dinner gathering of friends or family suddenly turning unpleasant, when one person gives a harsh word and the tension spreads—sometimes just as a dark undercurrent, sometimes breaking out into open strife. No matter how good the food is, you lose your appetite. Proverbs knows that scene:

"Better is a dinner of herbs where love is

than a fattened ox and hatred with it." (15:17)

In fact, an important aspect of this contrast is that one way can masquerade as something it's not. A dinner with a fattened ox would be a rich person's feast; it would appear to be the much better meal. But, as 14:8 says, "`The wisdom of the prudent is to discern his way"—and that discernment is needed because "the folly of fools is deceiving."

One especially enjoyable proverb speaks to the issue of deceptive appearances:

"Where there are no oxen, the manger is clean,

but abundant crops come by the strength of the ox." (**14:4**)

In other words, don't be deceived by the pleasing appearance of a clean barn; that means there's no hard work or productive labor going on, which would involve mud and sweat and dirty beasts! I can't help but transfer this thought to the way many of us so often want our houses always to appear neat and clean—which sometimes means we've pushed to the side the important relational "work" in which we, for example, allow the kitchen to get messed up by various helping hands, or we just don't mind if people see us in the midst of ongoing projects or games or whatever! There are better things than a clean manger.

In the end, if we are not the prudent ones who discern beyond appearances, we will be deceived not just in little, temporary things. On this subject, **verse 12** offers a familiar warning:

"There is a way that seems right to a man,

but its end is the way to death."

The deception happens step by step along folly's path. The book of Proverbs would call us to "give thought to our steps" (**v 15**), warning us that these steps are along one of two ways, leading either to life or to death.

Justice

A second key theme in this section is *justice*. It's a theme that has been implicit in previous chapters, but it begins to rise to more prominence, especially in light of the abuses of unrestrained fools. We passed over one particular stand-alone proverb toward the end of chapter 13 that, surrounded by all the talk of riches, seems to cry out for the poor:

"The fallow ground of the poor would yield much food,

   but it is swept away through injustice." (13:23)

Exactly what kind of injustice is in view here, and on whose part, is not clear; we're simply given a quick glimpse of rich potential swept away—and the poor left poor, with little food. We've read about poverty as the result of laziness or wickedness (recall, for example, 6:10-11 and 10:3-4). But we've also read of opposite scenarios (recall, for example, 10:2 or the better dinner of only herbs in 15:17).

Chapters 14 - 15 develop a clear concern for justice in relation to the "poor," simply defined in these contexts as people who don't have enough to meet their material needs. **14:20** makes a sad but often-true observation:

"The poor is disliked even by his neighbor,

   but the rich has many friends."

The very next proverb steps in and offers the value judgment we might long for after reading that verse. First came the ground-level observation; next comes wisdom's perspective, which gets to the heart:

"Whoever despises his neighbor is a sinner,

   but blessed is he who is generous to the poor." (**v 21**)

The ultimately revealing perspective on the issue of justice toward the poor comes a few verses later:

"Whoever oppresses a poor man insults his Maker,

   but he who is generous to the needy honors him." (**v 31**)

What a piercing glimpse of the way in which Proverbs rests in the truth of our Creator God, who set this world perfectly in order from the beginning. Even fallen, this is still our Father's world, and every human being in it is made in God's image, marred though that image has become. To oppress any human person, then, is to insult that person's Maker, the Lord God, whereas (by contrast) to be generous to one in need honors the Lord, showing care for all he has made. Again our relationship with God is front and center. This is no abstract law; how we treat what (or who) he has made is a very personal matter to God. Our Lord would call us to value each and every person based on his creation of us, not on our creature-limited evaluations.

> Our Lord calls us to value every person based on his creation of us, not on our creature-limited evaluations.

The people of Israel would have known that God included care for the poor in his revealed law. For example, Deuteronomy 15:7-11 explains in detail that if one of them should become poor in the land God was giving them, they were commanded not to harden their hearts or shut their hands, but rather: "You shall open wide your hand to your brother, to the needy and to the poor, in your land" (Deuteronomy 15:11). The context for all their generosity was God's repeated reminder of what he had done for them: "You shall remember that you were a slave in the land of Egypt, and the LORD your God redeemed you" (Deuteronomy 15:15).

The Old Testament context here in Proverbs is implicit, not explicit—although we never leave behind the book's introductory context of God's word and God's people (Proverbs 1:1). It is fascinating and wonderful that in these proverbs in chapter 14 the principles of generosity and justice for the poor stand firm on the foundation of God the Creator. That foundation is enough to demand justice. When we think of all the further depths of revelation, culminating in God's great gift of salvation to us in Christ his Son, we cannot even express how our generosity should overflow in thankful and merciful response.

The Heart

A third key theme in this section is the *heart*—basically the inner person: not simply our emotions but rather the core of our whole being.

Proverbs acknowledges our hearts. For all its practical emphasis, it includes the complexity of our deepest human experiences. We've noted already the connection between heart and words. In chapter 14, a few of the proverbs seem to stop and just look, with a kind of truthful compassion, into the human heart:

"The heart knows its own bitterness,
    and no stranger shares its joy." (**14:10**)

There's a comforting honesty here, as wisdom shines its light of observation all around, even inside people. It's true: no person around you knows just what it's like to experience the particular bitternesses and joys you carry in your heart. (Although to hear this truth stated is to have our personal experience acknowledged and somehow validated by the voice of wisdom. We'll come back to this.)

Proverbs' wisdom sees and says it from all angles. Yes, "a glad heart makes a cheerful face," and by contrast a sorrowful heart crushes the spirit (15:13). Then again, the outward evidence doesn't always tell the full story:

"Even in laughter the heart may ache,
    and the end of joy may be grief." (**14:13**)

Such proverbs not only speak truly into our personal experience; they also guard against too-easy assumptions concerning the people around us—particularly the assumption that we can understand what others are going through. Regularly—especially as I speak to various groups of women—I look out on an audience and just try to begin to imagine the depths of the sorrows, the joys, and the stories in process, that those women carry with them underneath the prepared faces that I can see lined up and ready for worship. And I know I can't.

But the Lord can. Proverbs lets us see with the Lord's eyes into the mysteries of the human heart. We see what happens when wisdom dwells there: "Wisdom rests in the heart of a man of understanding" (v 33a). The understanding heart is one that "seeks knowledge" (15:14a)—knowledge of the Lord whom we are called to fear.

Questions for reflection

1. What sparks anger, in your experience? List all the things you can observe about anger in 14:29.

2. In what ways does our view of God shape our view of the rich and the poor around us?

3. Which of the proverbs addressed in this section make you think about how you behave and talk when you're at home and with family?

PART TWO

The LORD

If we were to name a fourth key theme for this whole section, it would simply be the name *Yahweh*, "the LORD." We saw the fear of the Lord right away in 14:2, defining the foundational contrast. The presence of the Lord grows more and more prominent through chapters 14 and 15, pulling together the themes we've noted, and pulling them toward a climactic point in the first verses of chapter 16.

Proverbs **14:26** offers an inspiring glimpse of the fear of the Lord at work, generation after generation:

"In the fear of the LORD one has strong confidence,
  and his children will have a refuge."

Many of us will have seen this—believers passing on to children not just intellectual truth but also a personally trusted refuge in the Lord they fear. It doesn't always get passed on. But this proverb points the way; and it helps us pray, first for ourselves and then with trust in the Lord for those coming after us, that we and they might find this refuge and live in it.

Verse 27 is a great example of how the proverbs in general tend to swirl around us with significant repetitions (and changes). This verse repeats 13:14, with the same glorious image of the fountain of life—only here in chapter 14 "the teaching of the wise" is replaced with "the fear of the LORD." The two phrases are interchangeable, and one necessitates the other. Without the fear of the Lord we have no wisdom and no true life.

The foundational truth of the fear of the Lord keeps shining through, making all the difference. Remember that dinner of herbs with love, better than the fattened ox with hatred (**15:17**)? Right before that verse comes a corresponding "better than" proverb:

"Better is a little with the fear of the LORD
  than great treasure and trouble with it." (**v 16**)

So, before the specific example of the contrasting meals, first we are given the foundational perspective. The fear of the Lord is the issue at the heart of the contrast, Proverbs is telling us.

Consider the theme of justice. We saw the Creator God as the foundation of Proverbs' concern for justice and generosity toward the poor (14:31). In **15:25**, the Lord himself is named as the one acting in the cause of justice:

"The LORD tears down the house of the proud
  but maintains the widow's boundaries."

This proverb is fascinating in light of 14:1. How can this verse not remind us of that disturbing picture of folly tearing down her house with her own hands—but here the *Lord* is doing the tearing down. Which is it? Both. Human folly brings disastrous consequences—all under the hand of the sovereign God who made and rules all creation.

The Lord's rule is active: he is pictured here not only as tearing down the house of the proud (who are probably exploiting the widow); he is also, by contrast, maintaining the widow's boundaries. That is, he is watching over the most vulnerable and unprotected, even as the law declared: "He [the LORD] executes justice for the fatherless and the widow, and loves the sojourner, giving him food and clothing" (Deuteronomy 10:18). This is the truth made manifest in the story of Ruth and Naomi, who were widows and so were protected not only by laws allowing them to **glean** in the harvest fields but also by provisions for a **redeemer** who would care for them and their families (Ruth 2 – 4).

And this is the truth embodied by Jesus, who saw a poor widow putting her two small coins into the offering box, and who made sure that others saw her too—not just his disciples then but us now, as we read God's word (Luke 21:2). This word consistently shows us a Lord God who sees and rules it all:

"The eyes of the LORD are in every place,
  keeping watch on the evil and the good." (Proverbs **15:3**)

Consider the theme of the "heart." It is of course the Lord who sees the ways of the heart:

"Sheol and Abaddon lie open before the LORD;
    how much more the hearts of the children of man." (**v 11**)

Here is the clear explanation for that sense that even our private experiences are known by wisdom. It's the Lord at the beginning and end of it all—and at the heart of it all. "Sheol" and "Abaddon" refer to the realms of death and destruction—the dark places we human beings imagine and fear. They are closed off to us; they lie open only before the Lord—which makes us think not only of his sovereign knowledge but also of his sovereign judgment. The parallelism here shows "hearts" lying open before the Lord—which makes us think of the same divine qualities in relation to our deepest thoughts and desires.

Surrounding that proverb about hearts lying open are several proverbs again telling us about the Lord's personal response to us human beings as we walk one path or the other. He knows and judges our thoughts: "the thoughts of the wicked" are an "abomination" to him, but "gracious words," evidently coming from hearts that fear him, are "pure" (**v 26**). **Verse 8** contrasts the sacrifice of the wicked with the prayer of the upright: one is again "an abomination to the LORD" and the other is "acceptable to him." The very next verse again calls the way of the wicked "an abomination to the LORD"; by contrast, "he loves him who pursues righteousness" (**v 9**).

> As strong as God's judgment of evil is, stronger by contrast is his love for his people.

"He loves him"! Here is an affirmation not to be missed or overshadowed by the condemnations. As strong as God's judgment of evil is, so strong or stronger by contrast is his love for his people who fear him. Recall that figure of Wisdom calling and calling for us, telling us, "I love those who love me" and "Those who seek me diligently find me" (8:17). The love of the Lord is an eternal love and a personal love. It's the love our hearts seek and a love fully revealed in the Lord Jesus who laid down his life to save us from our sin.

The "Seam" in the Middle

We come now to a clear concentration of references to Yahweh, the LORD, here at the center of this collection. The commentator Lindsay Wilson calls the verses connecting chapters 15 and 16 a "theological seam in the middle" (*Proverbs*, page 22). We saw how the fear of the Lord held together the first nine chapters, introduced in the prologue (1:7) and appearing again climactically at the center point of chapter 9. We will see in the end how this concept unites the entire book. But even as we journey through, we find the Lord, and the fear of him, to be a strong thread that consistently holds the book together.

As chapters 14 and 15 pile up references to the Lord, he comes more and more clearly into view. **15:30-33** brings us to a dramatic point of promise: both **verse 30** and **verse 31** cease antithetic parallelism in order to point only positively to the light and life up ahead for those who will listen and walk wisdom's path. "Instruction" and "reproof" are both mentioned twice, as the substance of the life-giving message that turns us away from evil and toward the Lord.

The concentrated message to come, in **16:1-9**, is summed up well by chapter 15's final verse:

"The fear of the LORD is instruction in wisdom,
and humility comes before honor." (**15:33**)

In the first line's direct equation, the fear of the Lord *is* instruction in wisdom: fearing him is not to be separated from taking in wisdom's words. The parallel line tells us to position ourselves rightly: not like the proud, whose house the Lord tears down (**v 25**), but with humility that acknowledges the Lord and heeds his voice.

The first nine verses of chapter 16 develop the idea of humbly trusting the sovereign Lord. **Verse 1** and **verse 9** form matching bookends, each beginning with the heart of a man that lays his plans, and each setting alongside those plans the Lord's final word (**v 1b**) or final direction (**v 9b**).

Verse 2 reiterates the idea of God's sovereignty, this time in his supreme knowledge of us his creatures. We might think we judge ourselves rightly, for...

"All the ways of a man are pure in his own eyes,

but the LORD weighs the spirit."

In light of this sovereign Lord, there is but one command in this whole section telling us how to respond:

"Commit your work to the LORD,

and your plans will be established." (**v 3**)

This is no passive giving up before a sovereign God; rather, as Kidner points out, the verb "commit" pictures an action—literally to "roll," as in Psalm 37:5: "Commit your way to the LORD" (*Proverbs*, page 118). Proverbs calls us to the ultimately humble action of *rolling* our work (all our efforts) into the hands of the Lord—trusting him to "establish" our plans according to his sovereign plan.

Rolling something into someone else's hands (picture a ball) means that I have to let go. This doesn't mean that I don't work hard and lay plans; it does mean that I actively give that work and those plans into the hands of the Lord, who is God and who is good. What I commit to him might be a gathering I organized, or a career I planned for, or a marriage or family I envisioned in a certain way. God's way is often not what we envisioned. And yet, walking in relationship with him, fearing him, we find the path opening ahead of us, step by step. These words echo those words of wisdom given by the father to his son, back in 3:5-6:

"Trust in the LORD with all your heart,

and do not lean on your own understanding.

In all your ways acknowledge him,
and he will make straight your paths."

The Problem of Iniquity

Proverbs' call to trust and commit to the Lord comes embedded in the complexity of this fallen world. The middle three verses of this section address head-on the reality of sin and the need for that sin to be dealt with.

Three truths about sin emerge clearly. First, sin is not outside of God's sovereign control. It's hard for us to understand the affirmation of **16:4**: "The LORD has made everything for its purpose, / even the wicked for the day of trouble." This does not mean that God is the author of sin, but it does mean that he is sovereign over it, and that his purposes prevail through it. The believers in the early church prayed to their "Sovereign Lord," affirming that **Herod** and **Pontius Pilate** and others had gathered against Jesus "to do whatever your hand and your plan had predestined to take place" (Acts 4:24-28). What a strangely comforting truth: that in the evil we see around us, we can know that God's purposes prevail.

The second truth about sin is that it will be punished:

"Everyone who is arrogant in heart is an abomination to the LORD;
be assured, he will not go unpunished." (Proverbs **16:5**)

This arrogance of heart is the opposite of the humility in a heart that fears the Lord (see **15:33**). How revealing that it's not an evil action receiving punishment here, but rather an evil heart—the heart being the inner source of all our actions, and the deep place where we either fear God or reject him. If the arrogant in heart looks like he's prospering now, don't worry, says Proverbs; punishment will surely come—a punishment that is not defined here (although we have seen the Lord who tears down the house of the proud, in **15:25**).

The third truth about sin in this passage is the most startling, and ultimately the most comforting. It is that sin is **atoned** for, in a certain way:

"By steadfast love and faithfulness **iniquity** is atoned for,
and by the fear of the LORD one turns away from evil." (**16:6**)

Some commentators attribute this "steadfast love" and "faithfulness" to the righteous person who fears the Lord. **Verse 2**, however, has already warned us that, even when a man's ways are pure in his own eyes, the Lord "weighs the spirit." The kind of wickedness we've seen in **verses 4-5** will demand atonement that is greater, it seems, than any man would be capable of providing—unless that man were somehow perfectly righteous in the Lord's eyes.

"Steadfast love and faithfulness" have appeared before; 14:22 pictured those who "devise good" as meeting steadfast love and faithfulness along their path. These two qualities actually would have been utterly familiar to the Israelites who had heard God's word, for these are the words repeatedly used to describe the Lord's own covenant love for his people (see, for example, Exodus 34:6; Numbers 14:18-19; Psalm 33:18-22).

It was indeed through the Lord's steadfast love for his people that he mercifully provided a way for their sins to be forgiven, or atoned for—for centuries through the system of temple sacrifices established in the ceremonial law, but ultimately through the one perfect sacrifice to which all those other sacrifices pointed. Through the blood of Jesus, the sinless Son of God, our sin was finally atoned for, as Jesus himself took the punishment for our sin in our place on the cross (Romans 3:22b-26; Hebrews 10:12-14). When we by faith trust in Christ for the forgiveness of our sins, we are experiencing the full and final meaning of Proverbs **16:6**.

Walking in the Light

The parallel line of verse 6 proceeds to the results of this atoning work: a life lived in the fear of the Lord, turning away from evil. These verses in chapter 16 have invited us to follow what we might call a "gospel train of thought": we are called to trust the sovereign Lord God; we are confronted with our sin and the punishment we deserve; we find atonement for that sin in God's steadfast love and faithfulness; finally, we walk in relationship with him.

This is, obviously, the gospel still veiled in its Old Testament context, before all God's promises of steadfast love were revealed in Christ. And yet it is gospel truth, grounded in those promises and in the character of the Lord who is the same yesterday, today, and forever.

Verses 7-9 exude the blessings of a righteous life: that is, a life lived in the fear of the Lord. This person actually pleases the Lord, and lives in peace (**v 7**). Even if such God-fearers are not materially rich, their "little with righteousness" is better than "great revenues with injustice" (**v 8**). Interestingly, here it's the one with little who lives out justice. You don't have to be rich to live in a way that honors the poor.

When we finally come to **verse 9**, with the repeated contrast between the heart of man that plans his way and the Lord who establishes his steps, we read those words with increased confidence and insight, having followed this gospel train of thought. We have been confronted again with our need and with God's provision through his steadfast love and faithfulness. And so we will be quicker to commit our way to him—to roll our very lives into his sovereign hands.

These verses mark the end of the steady use of antithetic parallelism that has characterized the first half of "The Proverbs of Solomon." After this center section, the proverbs use more varied forms—sometimes antithetic, sometimes synonymous, and often variations of synthetic parallelism, where the second line simply continues or develops the proverb's meaning. Perhaps it's the case that the contrast between wisdom and folly has to be made dramatically stark first, before we proceed to various other topics in subsequent chapters.

In any case, as we move on, we do so with the foundation of wisdom, the fear of the Lord, utterly clear.

In England's Lake District National Park, driving through the steep mountainous area where the roads twist all around and up and down, I recall a series of signs warning of an especially dramatic descent ahead. After several informational signs noting the dangerous grade of the road to come, a final sign simply read, "YOU HAVE BEEN WARNED." If there's any chance that we might be tempted to take these proverbs as rules which we can grit our teeth about and obey in our own strength, or as promises that we'll benefit from if we're good enough, we have been warned.

At this point in Proverbs, we have been warned most of all about our hearts. We are so easily hard and proud of heart—perhaps especially some of us "good," "moral" folks. Proverbs insistently reminds us of a sovereign Lord who sees and judges our hearts, but who in mercy calls us to himself and lovingly leads us along the path of life rather than death. We have been warned about the two paths. And we have been invited to fear the Lord and humbly follow the path of life.

Questions for reflection

1. Was there a particular time when you learned more of what Proverbs means when it says that our hearts make our plans but the Lord establishes our steps?

2. What does it mean, in your circumstances, to "commit your work to the Lord"?

3. What truths about the Lord in Proverbs 16:1-9 give you comfort and joy? How do those truths point you to Christ?

8. LIVING IN THE CONTRASTS

We've seen the first half of "The Proverbs of Solomon," which sets up the contrasts between wisdom and folly. We've been reminded of the fear of the Lord, which makes all the difference. Now we're ready to move into the second half of this section, which shows what it's like to live in the contrasts. We'll first examine the rest of chapter 16, which looks realistically but hopefully ahead. Then we'll peer into chapters 17 – 19, where evil might threaten to over-whelm—but doesn't.

First, a King

After the middle "seam" of 16:1-9, which focuses on the Lord, we come to a section that focuses on a king (**v 10-15**). We most naturally think of the king mentioned in 1:1: "Solomon, son of David, king of Israel." Proverbs' context points us to a king (and a kingly line) established by God for his people, so that the king would lead them according to the Lord's revealed word.

In 16:1-9 we looked up to the sovereign Lord of heaven, who rules and judges all. Now we're looking up not only to the Lord but also to the throne he established. **Verse 11** reminds us of the perfectly just Ruler *above* the earthly king; but it is also telling us about this king, for it shows the "just balance and scales" which judge even the king, who is to represent God's justice to the people.

This verse might give an ironic tinge to the other verses extolling the righteousness of the earthly king. In **verse 10**, the king has an "oracle" on his lips: he brings the word of the Lord. King David and King Solomon had the law written down by Moses, and God continued to give his word not only through prophets but also directly to these kings. When **verse 10** goes on to say that the king's "mouth does not sin in judgment," we understand that this is the king's calling: to rule righteously according to God's word. Of course, even if we know only the stories of David and Solomon, we know that these kings sinned in all kinds of ways.

Verse 12 continues to address the nature of kingship: "It is an abomination to kings to do evil." This word "abomination" has consistently expressed God's judgment of evil (11:1, 20; 12:22; 15:8, 9, 26; 16:5). Along with **verse 11**, then, **verse 12** hangs God's perfect judgment right over the head of a king, who should not do evil because "the throne is established by righteousness." The *Lord's* righteousness is in view—a righteousness that is meant to be reflected by his **anointed** king.

Proverbs does not stop to tell the stories of kings' sins; that is for other parts of Scripture (see, for example, 2 Samuel 11 and 24; 1 Kings 11). These lines clarify the order of authority and then make some observations about that authority as it is carried out (or not). Proverbs **16:13-15** shows a king's interactions with his subjects: the king delights in "righteous lips" and loves "him who speaks what is *right*" (my emphasis)—just as does the Lord God, who established the throne in *righteousness*.

In fact, these verses tell us truth about God's king that is also truth about God: the king loves true words (**v 13**); his wrath brings death and must be appeased (**v 14**). And **verse 15** is too beautiful not to quote in full:

"In the light of a king's face there is life,
    and his favor is like the clouds that bring the spring rain."

Verses 10-15 apply to the king the truths revealed in verses 1-9 about the Lord himself: the sovereign judge who will punish iniquity—iniquity that must be atoned for to make way for righteousness and peace.

What shall we twenty-first century readers do with these verses about a king? Many earthly kings and queens have come and gone, none coming even as close as did David and Solomon to the sinless judgment Proverbs describes. One of the painful realities of our modern world is the detailed public exposure, through the media, of the gross sins of all kinds of political rulers. How we long for a righteous ruler!

God had promised David that in his line would come a king whose throne would be established forever (2 Samuel 7:12-16). For centuries, God's people looked and longed for that king—even when after Solomon their kingdom was divided and destroyed, and even when they eventually came under the rule of godless kings and empires.

Living after the coming of King Jesus, we Christians know that the true king in the line of David has come. What is true about God is perfectly true about this king. This king died, offering himself as the perfect sacrifice to appease God's wrath for sinful people. And this king rose from the grave to reign forever—and he is coming again to judge all, in perfect righteousness. Our New Testament perspective shines full light on the yearned-for king—a king not of one nation but of a people from all the nations. For the readers in King Solomon's time and subsequently, these verses must have increased both their yearning and their faith. These verses call all readers to look up in faith to the throne of such a king, whose favor brings life and light to the whole earth.

Walking On, Knowing What Is Better

Following Proverbs 16's sections on the Lord and the king, our gaze comes down to the pathway (or "highway," **v 17**) that we're called to keep walking, in the light of the truths we've seen. **Verses 16-19** contain two "better than" proverbs, of which we've already seen several (15:16, 17; 16:8). **Verse 16** establishes a contrast within one line: "How much better to get wisdom than gold!" and then makes a synonymous contrast in the second: "To get understanding is to be chosen rather than silver." These lines sum up the call to wisdom from the book's early chapters (see 2:4; 3:14-16; 8:10-11), continuing the imagery of precious jewels to point to the even greater value of wisdom—and driving the point home with the double punch of antithetic contrast and synonymous emphasis all within one proverb.

Verses 18-19 deliver another series of punches, with the first proverb giving a double warning against pride, and the next showing humility with poverty as "better" than pride with riches. We previously encountered **verse 18** as an example of synonymous parallelism; it is helpful here to put that verse together with its mate, which points to the contrasting positive virtue even while comparing it with another negative example of pride. The introduction of poverty and riches into the comparison adds yet another layer of complication; these challenges of character are not simple formulas, but truths to be worked out in the midst of real-life complexities.

These verses show us what is better. Indeed, to get wisdom is better than anything else, even gold or silver (**v 16**). To seek that wisdom with humility, with a lowly spirit, is better—better than pride, even pride with a lot of riches. For pride goes before destruction, and riches are worthless before the wrath of the Lord, to whom a person arrogant in heart is an abomination (**v 5**). Proverbs could not be more consistent in its message.

Walking On, Seeing the Two Ways

The rest of chapter 16 shows the two pathways, not with antithetic parallelism that sets up the contrast within individual proverbs but with two clumps of proverbs that take us down wisdom's path, and then folly's.

Guess what issue distinguishes first the wise, and then the fools? *Words.* **Verses 20-24** wonderfully describe words from the wise, and **verses 26-30** tell the opposite story. Although the presenting issue is speech, these sections describe two dramatically contrasting kinds of people, who differ both inside and out.

Verse 20 appropriately comes first in the first clump: it tells the source of the wise person's good words. The phrase "gives thought to the word" has been variously interpreted; it seems sensible to understand the parallel lines together, with the "word" referring to the word of the Lord, in whom this blessed person is trusting. In 13:13 we saw that "the word" was parallel to "the commandment." The source of the words described here, then, is a heart that fears the Lord and listens to his word—a heart of wisdom.

Indeed, **16:21** describes the "wise of heart," who is called "discerning" and whose "sweetness of speech increases persuasiveness." Both **verse 21** and **verse 23** mention this "persuasiveness." Both verses also stress the heart of the wise: evidently a heart that discerns what is in the hearts of others and what words will effectively draw them into the good path. There's nothing wrong with words that persuade when they come from a wise heart.

"Sweetness" of speech is also mentioned twice (**v 21, 24**). In **verse 24**, this sweetness is parallel to "gracious words"—that is, words offered from a gracious heart and in a way that expresses grace to the receiver. This means words that are carefully chosen in order to draw a person toward life and away from death. This verse pictures these gracious words as a honeycomb, bringing both sweetness to the soul and health to the body.

I often think of Abigail in relation to such verses. Abigail makes a brief but dramatic appearance in 1 Samuel 25, when David (anointed but not yet king) is incensed at Abigail's foolish husband Nabal for refusing to share provisions with David's band of men out in the wilderness, hunted by King Saul. David is about to bring his men to destroy Nabal's household when Abigail shows up out in the wilderness on a donkey, along with a lot of donkeys laden with abundant provisions. It's an electric moment, as Abigail sees David, gets down from her donkey, bows low to the ground, and gives one of the most discerning, persuasive, judicious, gracious, and full-of-sweetness speeches in the Bible (1 Samuel 25:24-31). Here is a woman who tells the truth in the most disarming manner. She could have self-righteously reproached David: *What on earth are you doing?* Instead, she calls David to remember the Lord's faithfulness and the Lord's word. And she does it humbly and beautifully, weaving in figures of speech that would have pierced the heart of David the poet.

Words like honey can be dangerous, when they are on the tongue of a fool (recall Proverbs 5:3-5). But on the lips of a God-fearer, gracious words like a honeycomb bring life. In 1 Samuel 25, David's soul is indeed pierced by Abigail's wise words. As a result the Lord's anointed is restrained from sinful revenge, and a whole household is saved.

> Is it as true for you as it is for me that your words are often the thing you regret at the end of a day?

How often do you ponder and pray about your words? Is it as true for you as it is for me that your words are often the thing you regret at the end of a day? For me, it is not just words spoken; I also often regret the words of grace I did not speak. Gracious words I didn't offer to an angry person—whom I allowed to make me angry, too. Gracious words I didn't give to a frazzled store clerk—who surely could have used a moment of grace. Gracious words I didn't share with a person heading into sin—who might by God's grace have turned from that sin.

The Other Way—And the Point

In the middle of this clump of proverbs on good words comes one line of warning. After celebrating "good sense" as a "fountain of life," Proverbs **16:22** reminds us that, by contrast, "the instruction of fools is folly." Proverbs never lets us forget the reality of that other way first introduced in 1:7b. The "good clump" (**16:20-24**) is followed by a "bad clump" (**v 26-30**).

Between the clumps comes a proverb that turns the corner. Verse 25 repeats 14:12, reminding us that "there is a way that seems right to a man"—a way that leads to death. Placed here, the proverb seems to warn us not to assume that we are the "good people" but rather to take a careful look at evil, examining our lives to see if any "turning aside from evil" is called for (**16:17**).

Verses 26-30 vividly describe persons of foolish words, not motivated by a wise heart but driven by "appetite" (**v 26**)—surely implying all kinds of appetites: for food, money, pleasure, revenge, and so forth. Unlike the lazy person who does nothing, this person is a "worker" who does a lot—a lot of harm. The descriptions of who this person *is*—"worthless man" (**v 27a**), "dishonest man" (**v 28a**), "man of violence" (**v 29a**)—are matched by the descriptions of what he *does*. He's busy plotting evil, with speech like "scorching fire" (**v 27b**); spreading strife and whispers that separate close friends (**v 28**); enticing his neighbor to evil (**v 29**). **Verse 30**, with the dishonest winking and the pursing of lips, recalls the similarly described man in **6:12-15**, whose whole body is jerking like a marionette's, contorted by evil that harms others and eventually breaks him beyond healing.

What a contrast to the sweetness of the one who is wise in heart and words! The two paths are laid out with great impact, as the lines and the proverbs build, one clump showing up the other. These intense views of both ways surely mean to intensify our will to go the better way.

The chapter's final three proverbs point again toward that better way. As a person with increasingly gray hair, I love **16:31**! This verse urges the reader toward perseverance along the path of wisdom, promising the gift of long life that will be enjoyed and celebrated:

"Gray hair is a crown of glory;
    it is gained in a righteous life."

And after all the violent harm we've just witnessed in **verses 26-30**, we are ready to believe the dramatic claim of **verse 32**: that a person who is slow to anger is indeed "better than" the mighty, and one who rules his spirit than one who takes a city. To meet the kinds of evil we've seen, we will need strength greater than anything we can see; we will need inner, spiritual strength.

The final point takes us back to the starting point: the One who oversees all people and paths, and the only source of the strength of spirit needed to follow wisdom's path. We end this whole section by looking up once more, above the paths, to the sovereign Lord we are called to fear and trust:

"The lot is cast into the lap,
    but its every decision is from the LORD." (**v 33**)

Questions for reflection

1. As we navigate the good and evil around and within, why do we so need humility (and why do we so fight pride)?

2. Do you pray about your words? How and what and when should we pray about our words?

3. How can we teach those coming after us not to focus only on good and evil actions but also (and most importantly) on the heart?

PART TWO

Walking On, in Real Life

We'll discuss chapters 17 – 19 in less detail, dipping in enough to get a sense of the varied assortment of proverbs. A few clumps stand out, but in general there is even more jumping from one topic to another—just like real life! These chapters communicate less overall optimism and more of the feel of plowing through the realities of yesterday and tomorrow.

About half the proverbs in these chapters offer purely negative observations about foolish behavior. The ones offering unqualified positive observations are few and far between; they do stand out. Some observations give two sides. Some involve no overt judgment. Not until we get toward the end of chapter 19 will we find another clearly positive section that lifts our eyes to the Lord.

We should appreciate progressions of proverbs like these. Often we go through a week that feels just like these chapters, with a lot of hard things and only a few rays of light to remind us of what we believe beyond what we can see. These chapters remind us to see straight, to walk straight, and to hope.

For each chapter we will ask two questions. First, *what folly is exposed?* Second, *what wisdom shines forth?*

Wisdom in the Midst of Strife

What folly is exposed? It's not easy to pull these chapters together thematically, but here's one truth about chapter 17: it exposes the folly of "strife."

Proverbs **17:1** introduces the theme of strife with a "better than" saying—a kind of parallelism we know by now. This one reminds us again of the dinner of herbs with love that is better than a fattened ox with hatred (15:17). We keep coming back to the table in Proverbs, just like we do every day of our lives. As we gather for a meal, the relationships around the table determine the whole experience. Here, "a dry morsel with quiet" is better than "a house full of feasting with strife" (**17:1**). Picture the bare-bones meal around a peaceful table, and by contrast the busy kitchen full of rich food and a lot of biting comments.

With all its astute observations, this chapter has just one command. It's a command relating to strife and vividly communicating how strife looks and feels:

"The beginning of strife is like letting out water,
so quit before the quarrel breaks out." (**v 14**)

The NIV translates this proverb as "Starting a quarrel is like breaching a dam…" At first there's just a trickle, from a little hole, but it doesn't take long before the water that is meant to be contained is streaming out of control. There is that moment in a tense conversation when you know that if you give one more retort, the fight will be on—but if you stop, you can avoid an outright quarrel. "So quit"!

Verse 19 makes a telling judgment: "Whoever loves transgression loves strife." In other words, the love of strife is connected at heart to a cherished sinful rebellion against God. The parallel line pictures one who "makes his door high," proudly building a lofty entrance to his house, which is basically a barrier against people. One who lives in strife isolates himself from others and ultimately from the Lord his Maker, against whom, however, no door is high enough to prevent the coming destruction this verse declares.

Proverbs 17 shows many relationships in various stages of discord and strife. In verse 5 there is one who mocks the poor (and insults his Maker), and one who is glad at the calamity of others. The fool, who in his folly is worse than a "she-bear robbed of her cubs" (**v 12**), lurks disturbingly among these proverbs, ready to destroy anyone in the way. People return evil for good (**v 13**); bribes abound, making the wicked prosper and perverting the way of justice (**v 8, 23**).

Much is out of order in this chapter. It does not seem to us immoral for a wise servant to rule over a shameful son (**v 2**), and yet this turn-about represents a family order that has gone wrong due to a son's foolishness. **Verse 21** and **verse 25** comment sorrowfully on such a situation, letting us see that "a foolish son is a grief to his father" and "bitterness" to his mother. It does not seem immoral for fools to speak with elegant language, and yet "fine speech is not becoming to a fool" (**v 7a**). Beautiful words on the lips of an evil man, or a fool with money in his hand to buy wisdom (**v 16**), are out of order.

Second, *what wisdom shines forth*? Amid all the disorder and strife of broken relationships, it is through faithful relationships that wisdom shines. I don't think it is just because I'm a grandmother that **verse 6** positively leaps out of the text, surrounded as it is by negative observations. This verse pictures another crown (as in 16:31), also for older people—this

> It is through faithful relationships that wisdom shines.

time made of grandchildren, who are "the crown of the aged." The parallel line jumps down the generations to the children and looks up to find glory in their fathers. We are meant to remember the father in chapters 1 – 9, who faithfully called his son to hear wisdom. **17:6** therefore shines brightly, insisting on the possibility and the goodness of generational faithfulness, even with examples of the opposite dotting the landscape.

Verse 17 also points to the beauty of relationships that are characterized by the opposite of strife and folly:

"A friend loves at all times,
　　and a brother is born for adversity."

In its simplicity, this proverb affirms the relationship of love and unselfishness between friends and brothers. "At all times" and "adversity" imply that the relationship will be tested but will endure strong under pressure of hardship. It's a proverb that calmly stands out in the midst of the strife filling much of this chapter—even strife that sometimes separates close friends (**v 9**).

The chapter does not let us put our hope simply in faithful human relationships. The book's Yahweh-centered perspective looms large over groups of proverbs like these. And among these proverbs the Lord is not absent; he is named twice—testing hearts (**v 3**) and calling an "abomination" both those who justify the wicked and those who condemn the righteous (**v 15**). The Lord sees, judges, and rules over all the disorder that has invaded his perfect creation. When evil and calamity are said to be coming for the wicked (as in **v 5, 11, 13, 19, 20**), we know that such evil and calamity are not separate from the Lord's sovereign purposes (see 16:1-5).

There are little glimpses of wise people living out their lives. There's the "man of understanding" into whom a rebuke goes deep (**17:10**). There's the joyful heart that is good medicine, presumably both for that person and for those around him—although the light of that line quickly disappears, darkened by its heartbreakingly true parallel: "but a crushed spirit dries up the bones" (**v 22**; see also 18:14). **17:27** shows people of knowledge and understanding who restrain their words and their spirit; this unreservedly good glimpse of wisdom lived out comes as a relief at the chapter's end.

The chapter's final verse finishes with tongue in cheek, with one of my favorite proverbs, and one that is surely good for all of us to remember:

"Even a fool who keeps silent is considered wise;
  when he closes his lips, he is deemed intelligent." (**v 28**)

Strong Evil, Stronger Hope

In chapter 18, *what folly is exposed*? After the positive glimpse of restrained words in the final verses of chapter 17, chapter 18 begins with a battering of proverbs that expose the folly of a fool's words. The kinds of people and words we saw back in 16:26-30 are still active and harmful; they always are. Foolish lips all around are walking "into a fight" (**18:6a**).

Today, we have only to peek at a few trending Twitter feeds to see how words are thrown back and forth like weapons—even with a word limit. (I think the word limit makes people sharpen their swords.) More than one public Christian figure has had to apologize publicly for words posted in haste or anger. If we think Proverbs' repeated attention to words is a little over the top, all we have to do is glance at social media's quickly multiplying excesses (or at the words we spoke last time we were annoyed with a friend).

In the opening string of chapter 18's negative observations, nearly every other one addresses the subject of words (**v 2, 4, 6, 7, 8**). The effect is that the evil mentioned in the alternate proverbs (**v 1, 3, 5**) becomes easily associated with people who use words as the surrounding proverbs describe. If we are people of foolish words, we are fools who will show our wickedness in a variety of ways. Evil is not just separate bad acts; evil is what grows from a sinful heart. Even in its darker passages, Proverbs is not just observing; it is instructing us about wisdom and folly and the human heart.

We all know the person described in **verse 2**:

"A fool takes no pleasure in understanding,
but only in expressing his opinion."

Have you ever been in a discussion group where this really irritating person just keeps talking? What a great warning for all of us to do more listening than talking! Indeed, giving an answer without really listening is "folly and shame" (**v 13**). James exhorts us clearly: "Let every person be quick to hear, slow to speak, slow to anger" (James 1:19).

Proverbs consistently makes clear the depth of this issue; it's connected to the life-and-death distinction of the two ways. A fool's words are his "ruin," and "his lips are a snare to his soul" (Proverbs **18:7**). Later in the chapter comes what might be Proverbs' strongest verdict on the power of words:

"Death and life are in the power of the tongue,
and those who love it will eat its fruits." (**v 21**)

Words can scorch like fire or bring sweetness to a soul (16:27, 24). They can be deep waters that destroy—or a fountain of wisdom that brings life (**18:4**; 16:22). They can be poisonous slander that tastes like delicious morsels but goes down deep and destroys relationships (16:28; **17:9**; **18:8**). Or they can be the carriers of life—as in that "word" of 16:20, which will bring us good when we take it in. Proverbs' call to "hear" wisdom is a call to take in life-giving good words, wisdom's words, God's words. And Proverbs calls us to speak words full of the wisdom we have received from the Lord.

Other kinds of folly show up in chapter 18—for example, the folly of trusting in wealth, imagining it to be your "strong city" or "high wall" (**18:11**). Many proverbs appear just as observations (with judgment only implied). **Verse 11** is like that: here's how a rich man imagines his wealth. **Verse 16** simply observes that a gift "makes room" for you, giving access to "the great." Perhaps a positive light on gifts is reflected here; with Proverbs' numerous mentions of bribes, however (see 15:27; **17:8, 23**), one might recognize them in this verse. Reading the proverbs in context teaches us to observe behavior around us and make discerning judgments.

What wisdom shines forth in chapter 18? Right before **18:11**'s rich man whose wealth is his "strong city" comes a marvelous picture of true (not imagined) security, found in Yahweh, the Lord:

"The name of the LORD is a strong tower;

the righteous man runs into it and is safe." (**v 10**)

Like a strong tower stands out against the landscape, such verses stand out in this chapter. **Verse 15** stands out as well, like a wise person surrounded by fools; the synonymous parallelism shows us one always "acquiring" and "seeking" knowledge, persevering along the good path.

Hope shines forth again through relationships, with the Lord and with family and friends. **18:22** is often quoted, telling us that finding a wife is finding "a good thing" and means receiving "favor from the LORD" (see 12:4; **19:14**). Actually, we do well to quote this verse these days, with the marriage rate declining among rising generations. It's not that everyone should get married. But the truth is that marriage is a good gift from the Lord, to be looked for and received with open hearts. As we celebrate the gift of marriage, in light of the Scriptures, we grasp more of the truths that God, through marriage, is showing us about himself and his love for us. All these relationships are intertwined.

In the chapter's final verse, one more person emerges from the crowd: a friend who "sticks closer than a brother" (**18:24**). Proverbs consistently elevates the value of faithful friendship (see **17:17**). "Friend" in Proverbs is not a verb—an action accomplished with the push of a button; "friend" is a noun—a person in the flesh who actually sticks by you and loves you along the pathway, in joys and in adversity.

Clouds With Breaks

In chapter 19, *what folly is exposed?* The first 15 verses of chapter 19 are mostly negative. **19:1** is a "better than" proverb that lets us glimpse "a poor person who walks in his integrity," but that person is quickly displaced by the fool in the parallel line (and subsequent lines). The only mention of the Lord in these verses comes with the fool whose heart "rages against the LORD" when he meets ruin (**v 3**). There are friends, but they desert a poor man (**v 4, 7**) and put on a show of friendship to a generous one (**v 6**).

What wisdom shines forth? There are breaks in the clouds. A person with "good sense" appears twice (**v 8, 11**), showing the qualities of wisdom and the benefits of those qualities. In **verse 14** there appears the "prudent wife" who is "from the LORD." But with **verse 16** the clouds seem to lift in a more comprehensive way, with a return to antithetic parallelism, which reminds us of the contrasting paths and how to find the good one. Along with 13:13 and 16:20, this proverb points us directly to the revealed word of God, that lights up wisdom's path:

"Whoever keeps the commandment keeps his life;

he who despises his ways will die." (**19:16**)

Verses 16-23 focus on the evidences of a life lived fearing the Lord and keeping his commandments: generosity to the poor, that "lends to the LORD" (**v 17**); discipline of a son, in which there is hope (**v 18**); and listening to instruction, "that you may gain wisdom in the future" (**v 20**). There is a looking ahead toward good things—a hope—along the path shown here. Even in this fallen world, where people are poor and children desperately need discipline, in following the word of wisdom from God there is hope.

That hope rests only in the Lord himself. This section lands on the most basic "Yahweh truths": "It is the purpose of the LORD that will stand" (**v 21b**); "The fear of the LORD leads to life" (**v 23a**). Whoever walks in that fear "rests satisfied," says **verse 23b**—ending this little section with a certain promise of "rest" ahead, but also now, along the hard path.

Some hard verses conclude this chapter. The path continues, and perseverance is required. The sluggard has none. He shows up here again in **verse 24** (and **v 15**)—so lazy that he can't even lift his hand from the dish to his mouth. We'll leave him stuck in that amusing pose and come back to him again; he'll still be there.

These final verses warn the one who might not listen to the word of instruction—the son who might not learn from a parent's discipline. Although **verse 25** reiterates that reproof will bring knowledge to a man of understanding, the subsequent verses picture a son who violently rejects his father and mother and who ceases to hear instruction—along with one who mocks at justice and a scoffer who deserves only condemnation (**v 26-29**).

This is what living in the contrasts is like. The good still shines out: the fear of the Lord in **verse 23** shines out bright—perhaps brighter in contrast to the evil around and within. It's important to see the evil and name it. It's most important to walk through it toward the light, walking in the fear of the Lord that leads to life.

Questions for reflection

1. Do these proverbs resonate with how your life has been going this week? If so, which ones stand out?

2. Describe one example of a faithful friend—an example you've seen up close.

3. Reflect on Jesus, the Son of God, walking through the world full of sin that is described in these proverbs. How did he show us the way?

9. THE SOLEMN REMAINDER OF SOLOMON

In this last part of "The Proverbs of Solomon," we'll look first at Proverbs 20:1 – 21:4 and then at 21:5 – 22:16. These chapters show a broadening arena of action (with increased attention given to the king); instructive synthesizing of the themes we've seen so far; and a consistent perspective acknowledging pervasive sin, righteousness in the midst of it, and the Lord's sovereign rule over all of it.

The King and Others

The king will make more of an appearance in these later chapters of "The Proverbs of Solomon." We saw the focus on the king in 16:10-15, immediately following the focus on the sovereign Lord (v 1-9). Chapter 19 compared the king's wrath to the growling of a lion—in contrast to his favor, which is like the dew on the grass (v 12). Here in chapter 20 it's the lion's growling that we hear again, signaling the "terror of a king" provoked to anger (**20:2**). In this verse his wrath is not mitigated by any contrast of his favor; in fact, the one provoking him "forfeits his life."

We'll meet the king again soon, but let's stop and note that these mentions of him mark an increasingly broadening arena of human behavior in Proverbs. Wisdom shines its light on the individual, the home and family, the neighborhood, the transactions of business, the realm of worship and sacrifice—and the entire kingdom, under the rule of a king. The ESV Study Bible notes that **verse 3** (coming after the warning of **verse 2**) may suggest that a king should himself learn to "keep aloof from strife," above the level of quarreling fools. In **verse 1**, positioned so near to the king's gaze and growl, we may picture the inebriated person as one who provokes the king to anger.

In that first verse, wine and strong drink themselves are called the "mocker" and the "brawler." These personifications of the misused alcohol show its potency; it takes over a person, who then has no chance of becoming wise. (We'll see more in Proverbs about drunkenness, including one extended passage in 31:4-7 explaining why kings themselves must not give themselves to wine or strong drink).

Who knows why we meet the sluggard here (**20:4**)? He's hanging around everywhere. We keep passing him as we make our way through the proverbs. We observe here his failure to plow his fields at plowing time (autumn), and his resulting "nothing" at harvest time. We'll meet him yet again in this section, experiencing the results of his laziness.

The King and the Lord

Verses 5-12 again view the king in light of the Lord. At first the point here seems to be that the king judges all; but ultimately, the point is that the Lord judges all, even the king. These proverbs can be meaningfully absorbed individually, but the context provides both clarification and depth to the meaning.

Verse 5 states the issue: "The purpose in a man's heart is like deep water"—perhaps simply suggesting that no one can see fully into the heart's depths, and perhaps also suggesting the darkness of sin (see 18:4). It takes a "man of understanding" to discern (or "draw out") what is hidden in a human heart. The problem is exacerbated by the fact that "many a man proclaims his own steadfast love" (**20:6a**); that is, many people say they are good, even good like God ("steadfast love," as we've seen, is a term expressing God's own covenant kindness and merciful love—see 16:6).

The parallel line breaks in: "But a faithful man who can find?" (**20:6b**). Lots of people say it. "Let's *see* it," says this verse in effect. Where is that faithful man? **Verse 7** stops to delight in that man: that "righteous" one who "walks in his integrity," and whose children after him are blessed! We're looking for that man.

And so is the king:

"A king who sits on the throne of judgment
winnows all evil with his eyes." (**v 8**)

Picture the great king high on a "throne of judgment," peering down deep into people's hearts and lives and "winnowing" the evil—separating it out like the wheat from the chaff. Under the gaze of such discerning eyes, **verse 9** asks:

"Who can say, 'I have made my heart pure;
I am clean from my sin'?"

Who can say that? No one. In Solomon's time the temple purifications and sacrifices for sin had to be carried out repeatedly, for no one stays clean from sin. The question of this verse echoes throughout time and throughout Scripture, and the answer continues to be "no one." "All have sinned and fall short of the glory of God" (Romans 3:23).

The question of Proverbs **20:9** echoes loud in this passage, even reaching the king sitting on his throne of judgment. **Verse 10** lifts our eyes to the only perfect judge, the Lord, who again declares "unequal weights" and "unequal measures" an abomination (see 11:1; 16:11; **20:23**). He sees and judges it all—hearts and words and actions. Even the seemingly small act of cheating in a business transaction draws his eye, and his ire.

In the end, despite hidden hearts and boastful words, actions give indisputable evidence as to the truth. Remember, the righteous "walks" in his integrity (**v 7**). Let's see it! This is the thrust also of **verse 11**:

"Even a child makes himself known by his acts,
by whether his conduct is pure and upright."

Yes, this proverb emphasizes the importance of teaching children well. But its main point seems to be that people's actions clearly reveal the state of their heart; if this is true for "even a child," suggests the verse, how much more must it be true for a grown man or woman?

We live our lives under "the eyes of the LORD," which are in every place (15:3); hearts and lives lie open before him (15:11). The eyes of the king winnowing the evil in **20:8** are like the Lord's eyes, for the king's judgment is to reflect God's. But **verse 12** inserts a reminder that all eyes (and ears) are made by the Lord. The king of heaven created it all and rules over it all.

This is King Solomon's collection. His words here implicitly acknowledge both his God-ordained calling and also his limitations as a sinful human being in need of the Lord—and his words encourage every person to consider the same perspectives. The ringing questions of **verse 6** and **verse 9** call us to acknowledge our sin. Rather than crushing us, however, they turn us to the Lord in heaven. By steadfast love and faithfulness iniquity is atoned for, we have read (16:6). We on this side of the cross know that our iniquity was atoned for finally and completely by the one perfectly faithful man, the King of heaven who came down to save us.

Proverbs calls us to fear and follow this merciful Lord, by faith in his word. It calls us to trust only his steadfast love and faithfulness, ultimately revealed in his Son, who showed us that faithful man. Committing our way to him, humbly walking the path of wisdom laid out by his word, you and I by God's grace can become faithful men and women—the ones looked for in this passage.

To Market We Go

Proverbs **20:13-19** takes us to the marketplace, where "bread" (**v 13, 17**) pictures the provision we all need and work for, day by day. These verses offer a series of observations and admonishments relating to the economic arena.

Verse 13 recalls the lazy sluggard. "Love not sleep," is the command—with a warning attached: "lest you come to poverty." The parallel line commands positively, "Open your eyes"—with a reward attached: "and you will have plenty of bread." We are to get up and work, for our bread!

How do you, or the people around you, view work? Work, in Scripture, is not a necessary evil but a fruitful good. The first one we see at work in the Bible is the Lord himself, who finished his work of creation in six days and then rested on the seventh (Genesis 2:2-3). Before the fall, God put Adam and Eve in the Garden of Eden "to work it and keep it" (Genesis 2:15). Created in our Maker's image, we human beings are called to work.

The following verses speak to the ones out working and doing business in a fallen world. The observation of Proverbs **20:14** will make many of us smile, especially if we (like much of the world) regularly find ourselves bargaining for a good deal. While we're negotiating to buy something, we call the offer "bad, bad," but having made the purchase, we go away boasting in the deal we got. The next verse perhaps comments on such verbal maneuvering, asserting that "lips of knowledge" (truthful lips) are more precious than "gold and abundance of costly stones" (**v 15**).

We've seen the principle of **verse 16** before, and we'll see it again (6:1; 27:13). The proverb here focuses on strangers and foreigners: that is, people outside the community of God's people. The one who makes himself liable for such people's debts is at risk: so, take his garment as a pledge if you're doing business with him. It helps to remember that this principle has nothing to do with attitudes toward strangers or giving generously to the poor; it concerns prudence versus imprudence in financial dealings involving debt. In fact, when we are free from imprudent debts, we are much freer and more able to give generously to those in need.

These proverbs assume a world of sin. There is deceit in business: bread gained by deceit tastes sweet but turns to gravel in the deceiver's mouth (**20:17**). Economic strife is mirrored on the level of political strife; **verse 18** assumes there will be war and says to wage it according to good counsel and wise guidance. **Verse 19** points out the slanderer who in every arena is "going about" revealing secrets and making trouble; don't associate with that "simple babbler," we're told.

> Proverbs doesn't sink down under evil. It faces it straight on, but it never loses hope.

These calls to wise prudence in a world of sin can strengthen us, especially in the darker passages of our lives when we have to deal with a lot of folly around us (and in us). Proverbs doesn't sink down under the evil. It faces it straight on and calls it by name. It sees this sinful world of disorder for what it is—fallen. And it never loses hope in the Lord who oversees all of it, to the end.

Wait for the Lord

Proverbs 20:20 – 21:4 reveals a world of sin, with an earthly king on the throne and a sovereign Lord in heaven. We find here another clump of "king-proverbs" embedded in an unusually dense clump of proverbs naming the Lord.

First, these verses show sin as a defiant embracing of evil. After the book's many calls to children to listen to parents, **20:20** is shocking, portraying one who "curses his father or mother" and whose "lamp will be put out in utter darkness." The "lamp" pictures his spirit within him; this is a picture of death, as that lamp is snuffed out like a candle. Likewise, **21:4** pictures a "lamp of the wicked," revealing the "sin" of "haughty eyes and a proud heart."

A hasty rush into sin is emphasized at several points, first in **20:21**:

"An inheritance gained hastily in the beginning
   will not be blessed in the end."

This may be the same person who cursed his father or mother; now he's grabbing the inheritance. He is Proverbs' equivalent of the foolish youth in the story Jesus tells, that younger son who went to his father and said, "Father, give me the share of property that is coming to me" (Luke 15:11-32).

Proverbs warns against all kinds of foolish haste that draws one into evil. Proverbs **20:22** addresses an impulse for revenge, and **verse 25** points out the "snare" of rash vows made without reflection. We often attribute to young people this sort of unwise haste—it is for good reason that this book worked (and works) to teach youth the wisdom of discipline and restraint. Remembering the comprehensive audience addressed in the prologue (1:1-7), however, and considering all the opportunities for rashness available to older people with time and means, how can we not all be humbled by this counsel? I know many older as well as younger people who have pressed "send" or "purchase" or "post" in a quick, unthinking, and long-regretted moment.

The wisdom of **20:22b** speaks to all such rash impulses: "Wait for the LORD, and he will deliver you." The next two proverbs also name the Lord, focusing on his judgment of unjust dealings (**v 23**; see also **v 10**) and his sovereign ordering of our steps (**v 24**). These three mentions of the Lord are like bright stop-lights in the way of foolish haste, telling us to look up and see his hand before we take things into our own.

Three mentions of the king connect him again to the Lord. First, a "wise king winnows the wicked" (**v 26**), seeing and judging evil as he was doing in **verse 8**—and as the Lord does in **verse 10** and **verse 23**. Second, the king is "preserved" or protected on every side by the very qualities associated with the Lord himself:

"Steadfast love and faithfulness preserve the king,
   and by steadfast love his throne is upheld." (**v 28**)

The third mention of the king directly affirms the Lord's sovereign rule: the king's heart is a "stream of water in the hand of the LORD," who "turns it wherever he will" (**21:1**). These verses first apply to King Solomon and to the line of David that God established and directed for his redemptive purposes which were to be fulfilled in Christ. But that picture of the stream of water in the Lord's hand should give us strong confidence in his sovereign direction of every ruler in all times (even now) according to his worldwide redemptive purposes in Christ. What truth for us to trust, even when we are living under unrighteous rulers who do not know the Lord, for they nevertheless serve under his sovereign hand.

These verses keep turning our hearts to the Lord. The Lord directs the course of a human heart (**v 1**). The Lord of the perfectly just scales "weighs the heart" (**v 2**; see **20:27**).

What is the Lord looking for in our hearts? The opposite of pride (**21:4**)—that is, a humble fear of the Lord and an openness to his word. He's looking for a heart that waits on him, and a life that shows that kind of heart. Verse 3 again says, *Let's see it!* (see **20:6, 7, 11**):

"To do righteousness and justice
    is more acceptable to the LORD than sacrifice." (**21:3**)

There is much more to read and ponder in this section. That's part of what we should take away: the need to stop and listen more carefully—in effect, to "wait for the LORD" (**20:22**). Before talking too quickly about ourselves, or acting too quickly to accomplish what we want, what if we pause, listen, ponder, pray, and ask what the Lord wants to accomplish in us and through us, according to his word?

Questions for reflection

1. These proverbs about sinful behavior might be thought depressing. What do you think wisdom would say about that?

2. Did you identify with any of the rush and rashness pinpointed in these verses? How does the call to "wait on the LORD" speak to you?

3. How do these verses reveal a sovereign Lord God—and why is that a comforting revelation?

PART TWO

The Landscape

After the three mentions of the Lord in the opening verses of chapter 21, the landscape becomes rather bleak, full of sin on all sides—yet with significant rays of light and with a final couple verses at the end of this collection that turn us explicitly again to the Lord.

Proverbs **21:5-7** brings to mind those wicked companions about whom the father first warned his son: the ones whose "feet run to evil" and who "make haste to shed blood" (1:16). Evil deeds and their results grow fast in these verses: first, in contrast to the diligent and their abundance, we glimpse the hasty, who will come only to poverty (**21:5**); next come lies that set a "snare of death" (**v 6**); next is violence that will sweep the perpetrators away (**v 7**). The rush to sin is met by a rush of consequences.

The instances of antithetic parallelism stand out, being much fewer in this part of Proverbs. In **verse 5** the contrast begins with the *positive* (the "diligent") and lands in the second line on the *negative* (the "hasty")—which then takes over completely, until **verse 8**, where the contrast begins with the *negative* (the "guilty") and lands in the second line on the *positive* (the "pure"):

"The way of the guilty is crooked,
   but the conduct of the pure is upright."

As we observe evil and destruction, it does bring a kind of relief to have started on good solid ground and to land there once again, affirming the upright conduct of the pure.

That Quarrelsome Wife

As the observations continue, we come upon a well-known figure: the quarrelsome wife (**v 9**). We passed her before, with her quarreling like "a continual dripping of rain" (19:13). This figure is like the sluggard: always irritatingly there. We pass these figures often. Each time we see this quarrelsome wife, we're given some dramatic comparison that shows how irritating she really is.

In chapter 21 come two "better than" proverbs; the "better" places show just how bad is the place shared with this woman:

"It is better to live in a corner of the housetop
   than in a house shared with a quarrelsome wife."

(**21:9**; see 25:24)

"It is better to live in a desert land
   than with a quarrelsome and fretful woman." (**21:19**)

The same Hebrew word is translated both "wife" and "woman"; both proverbs here probably refer to a wife, as the one a man is living with. Before we broaden the application let's start with wives—for surely it is not a mistake that fretting and argumentative wives are given particular notice in the pages of Scripture, and so those who are wives can humbly learn from this.

As a wife, I need to ask myself how all Proverbs' instructions concerning pride, anger, harsh words, and strife apply to me in all contexts of my life—including specifically my behavior as a wife. Is there bubbling inside me some resentment toward my husband, that breaks out in quarrelsome words? Do I respect and listen well to my husband, or am I quick to challenge? What comes regularly out of my mouth: unhappiness about what I wish were different, or thankfulness for what is and constructive ideas for what might be? Am I honest with my husband? Do I turn his thoughts to the Lord? How could I better contribute to making our home a place of peace?

Men who are husbands might take notice of these proverbs concerning wives and ask questions such as: How might I encourage my wife to have a peaceful heart? Or, in what ways have I *not* lovingly encouraged her, perhaps contributing to her discontent? Do I turn her thoughts to the Lord? How do all Proverbs' instructions concerning pride, anger, harsh words, and strife apply to me in all contexts of my life—including specifically my behavior as a husband?

We must stop to acknowledge that a quarrelsome spirit in a spouse, whether husband or wife, is an evil to be repented of by the contentious one and met with prayerful patience by the other. As we saw in the book's prologue (1:1-7), Proverbs reaches out to all of us, invading with God's wisdom all the contexts of our lives. For wives and husbands—or for those planning to be wives or husbands—these verses hold instruction.

It is effective instruction, given not through a positive command but evidently through the honest report of one who has lived in close quarters with the folly of another's quarrelsome heart. He is repulsed. He just wants to get away. If I tend to cause strife with the person I live with, it is good for me to imagine experiencing myself through that person's eyes.

It is even better to look up and imagine myself in the Lord's eyes:

"The Righteous One observes the house of the wicked;
    he throws the wicked down to ruin." (**21:12**)

The wicked are called wicked here by the Righteous One who sees and punishes them—the Lord (see 11:21). Wickedness does not exist independently or grow unrestrainedly; the Lord sovereignly oversees all that he has created. If I am a person full of strife, then I am striving ultimately against the Lord—and need to go back to the very beginning: fearing him.

Rewards

Proverbs 21 directs our gaze not only to present observations but to future expectations. This chapter continues Proverbs' connection of positive rewards with wisdom, and negative rewards with folly. We saw the contrast of "abundance" for the diligent versus death and destruction for the wicked (**21:5-7**). We saw the Righteous One who sees and who himself brings ruin on the wicked (**v 12**).

The prospect of coming judgments and rewards restores a sense of order in the midst of the disorder created by sin. The unjust will meet appropriate, sometimes ironic, justice:

"Whoever closes his ear to the cry of the poor

will himself call out and not be answered." (**v 13**)

The one who wanders from the way will find himself not free but stuck, resting "in the assembly of the dead" (**v 16**). The one who goes after riches (loving pleasure and wine and oil) will be poor, not rich (**v 17**); "precious treasure and oil are in a wise man's dwelling" (**v 20**).

The sluggard now appears again, and he also suffers consequences matching his folly (**v 25-26**). He is reaping no harvest (from the fields he refused to plow, in 20:4) but only the reward of his laziness: desire unmet, desire that is killing him. "All day long he craves and craves" (**21:26**; see 10:3). We should look back and remember that it is ultimately the "*soul* of the sluggard" (my emphasis) that "craves and gets nothing" (13:4). What a sad and horrible picture of the constant unmet soul-craving of one who does not fear the Lord.

Three proverbs together in this section show by contrast the rewards of the righteous. **21:21** is full of weighty words communicating the substance of wisdom's treasures:

"Whoever pursues righteousness and kindness

will find life, righteousness, and honor."

"Righteousness" in both lines shines forth; here the reward exactly matches the pursuit. "Kindness" is the word often translated "steadfast love." This verse rings with the truth of wisdom's words in Proverbs 8:17: "Those who seek me diligently find me." In light of all the Scriptures, we know that the One we find is Jesus our Savior, the perfectly righteous One.

The subsequent two proverbs show wisdom's strength to defeat an enemy's city (**21:22**) and to restrain a tongue (**v 23**). Which strength is greater? 16:32 told us: "He who rules his spirit" is better than "he who takes a city."

The chapter closes with solemn urging to give thought not just to the future but even more to the One who directs it. "Abomination" in **21:27** turns our thoughts to the Lord; actually, 15:8 told us directly that "the sacrifice of the wicked is an abomination to the LORD." The proverbs all together fill in all the blanks.

Two antithetic parallelisms contrast the wicked with the one who "hears" (**21:28**) and the one who "gives thought to his ways" (**v 29**). The call here is to stop and listen—and look up to the sovereign Lord. The point here is that nothing can stand against the Lord's good purposes: "no wisdom, no understanding, no counsel" (**v 30**). The chapter's final verse puts this grand truth in a battle context:

"The horse is made ready for the day of battle,
  but the victory belongs to the LORD." (**v 31**)

The Rich and the Poor—And Discipline

Approaching the end of Solomon's proverbs, we find much attention given to the rich and the poor. The first nine verses of Proverbs 22 juxtapose rich and poor in a variety of ways. At the start, riches are put down; they are lower in importance than a "good name" or "favor" (**22:1**). The point is to seek not riches but relationships—first with the Lord, who in Scripture is often the One in whose sight we find favor, or who grants favor in the sight of others.

Verse 2 puts the rich and the poor together to reiterate a truth we've heard several times: "The LORD is the maker of them all." Again, the point is to value people, for we are all created by God in his image. "Well, of course," we say. We know that. But we are warned not to be like the simple, who pay no heed to warnings (**v 3b**), and instead to be like the "prudent," who see and avoid danger (**v 3a**), and like the one who "guards his soul" to keep far from the "thorns and snares" along the way (**v 5**). These are powerful human temptations: to value riches over people and to value rich people over poor people. If we think we're not tempted in these ways, there's a good chance we're being simple, if not utterly foolish.

Right in the center of this section is the truth that adjusts our scale of values:

"The reward for humility and fear of the LORD
 is riches and honor and life." (**v 4**)

Here's another verse full of words communicating the weight and worth of wisdom's treasures. *The fear of the Lord* is the beginning, in a heart that humbly listens to his word. As that person walks the path of wisdom, that person finds great reward: riches are listed first, yes, but they flow into greater things: honor and *life*.

It is just after these verses that we find this famous instruction:

"Train up a child in the way he should go;
 even when he is old he will not depart from it." (**v 6**)

There *will* be thorns and snares, and we must help a young person learn to find the way—the way of wisdom grounded in the fear of the Lord. Proverbs (and all of Scripture) is here to help us learn, and to help us train.

To follow the instruction of **verse 6** is part of fearing the Lord. Wisdom would have us carry it out with hearts of humility (**v 4**), acknowledging God's sovereignty over the heart of every human being he has made, including the young person we are training. We cannot presume to know the steps that the Lord will establish for this child (16:9). In the context of this wisdom teaching, we understand this verse not as a promise but as a pattern that God established from the beginning, as parents teach their children to know and serve the Lord, passing on the faith from generation to generation.

> Proverbs is here to help us learn, and to help us train.

We follow God's word in a fallen world, invaded by sin. Proverbs makes that abundantly clear—even as **22:15** returns to the subject of training children: "Folly is bound up in the heart of a child." The problem of sinful hearts that we saw in 20:9 is deep; it begins in a mother's womb (Psalm 51:5). Wisdom advises "training" (Proverbs **22:6**) and "discipline" (**v 15**; see 19:18).

"The rod of discipline" in **22:15** may mean more than corporal discipline; a rod can picture direction and instruction, although in 23:13, the rod is clearly used for corporal discipline. Whatever our views on this specific disciplinary method, there is certainly no warrant here (or anywhere in Proverbs) for harshness or anger; discipline is a matter of love. 3:11-12 compared the Lord's discipline and reproof of those he loves to a father's discipline of the son in whom he delights. The point here is that children need discipline—including consequences for wrongdoing and also guidance and instruction in the way they should go.

Children's folly-bound hearts need the kind of regular, heart-felt teaching of God's word described in Deuteronomy 6:

"These words that I command you today shall be on your heart.
You shall teach them diligently to your children, and shall talk
of them when you sit in your house, and when you walk by the
way, and when you lie down, and when you rise." (v 7)

God uses his breathed-out word to speak to the hearts of sinful people young and old, and to turn them to himself as the Spirit applies that word. We New Testament believers get to pass on to the next generation the whole of the Scriptures, which reveal the fulfillment of all God's promises in Christ. As we pass on his word, we can trust God to accomplish what he purposes (Isaiah 55:11). In the end the victory belongs to the Lord.

Concluding the Proverbs of Solomon

But this section does not end in victory. Right after Proverbs **22:15**, where the discipline of a child offers hope, the final verse in this section—**verse 16**—takes us right back to the complexities of rich and poor: the oppression of the poor, and the poverty that will come to those oppressing them.

If we return to **verse 6**, where the training of a child also offers hope, we find the subsequent verses likewise take us right back to the complexities of rich and poor, with the rich ruling over the poor, and the borrower forced to be the slave of the lender (**v 7**). The sowing of injustice will reap calamity, we're warned (**v 8**). Things are not yet as they should be. This is the fallen world in which training and discipline must take place.

And yet Proverbs always shows the two sides. The proverb that brings closure both to **verses 7-9** and **verses 1-9** lands on the goodness of generosity and the blessing that will come to the one who "shares his bread with the poor" (**v 9**).

Between **verse 9** and **verse 15** comes a final smattering of proverbs that shows the spectrum of wisdom and folly we have encountered. First comes the scoffer, who has consistently been the proud villain refusing rebuke (9:7; 13:1; 15:12). When he is driven out, then "strife" and "quarreling" and "abuse" will end (**22:10**). That's quite a claim. The scoffer is one who, in his pride, not only rejects the fear of the Lord but mocks it. Wisdom cried out in the beginning, "How long will scoffers delight in their scoffing?" (1:22). Solomon's collection ends by looking toward the scoffer's punishment, which **21:11** says can teach wisdom to a simple person.

These final proverbs beautifully pull together themes from the previous ones. The theme of words of course makes an appearance: **22:11-12** reaffirms the constant connection between heart and words, with true or false words rewarded with good or evil not just from the king but also from the Lord himself (both of whom are pictured here again, one after the other, lifting our eyes to the throne in heaven).

One more time we pass the sluggard—still there (**v 13**). And he's still doing nothing—this time with a truly wonderful excuse, and one we will see again: *There's a lion in the street!*

Verse 14 reaches back to the first nine chapters, recalling the "forbidden woman" with her false, enticing words; her mouth is "a deep pit," and "he with whom the LORD is angry will fall into it." Her reappearance at this point reaffirms her role in the book; she is here not only to show the very real evil of adultery but also to picture the way folly entices us away from wisdom's path. These proverbs have lit up the two ways, and the adulteress offers a final, vivid warning about the path of folly that leads to death.

We finish the first collection soberly, seeing the path of folly, but with hope as we hear the call to wisdom's path—and the call to train others to walk that path after us. The path of wisdom invites us, generation by generation, as we fear the Lord and heed his word.

Questions for reflection

1. What about that quarrelsome wife? What can you learn from her?

2. Whatever your situation in life, how can you hear and follow the call to train up the next generation to fear and follow the Lord?

3. How does having a "bountiful eye" and sharing bread with the poor (22:9) connect to God's care for us, his creatures—and ultimately his redemption of us through his Son?

10. THIRTY SAYINGS OF THE WISE— AND MORE

A new collection is introduced in Proverbs **22:17**: "Words of the Wise." Many of these proverbs are closely related to an earlier Egyptian wisdom collection titled "*Instructions of Amenemope*"; evidence suggests that Solomon (or wise men under Solomon's direction) may have borrowed and adapted sections from this Egyptian source (Wilson, *Proverbs: An Introduction and Commentary*, page 4). The adaptation grounds this wisdom in the fear of the Lord, shaping general revelation accessible to all into specific revelation made alive by the breath of God. We'll look first at 22:17 – 23:11, and then at 23:12 – 24:34 (which includes the added section "More Sayings of the Wise").

New Call—Same Point

Should it make us uncomfortable that these inspired writings overlap with secular ones? No; it should make us even more mindful of the one source of truth, the Lord who is the Maker of us all. Solomon was able to discuss wisdom with non-Israelites in the ancient world—as he did, for instance, with the queen of Sheba, who heard of Solomon's wisdom and paid him a visit (1 Kings 10:1-10). His wise answers to all her hard questions took her breath away (10:5) and gave her a glimpse, beyond Solomon, of "the LORD your God, who has delighted in you and set you on the throne of Israel ... that you may execute justice and righteousness" (10:9).

Scripture tells us that the wisdom God gave Solomon surpassed the wisdom of all the people of the east and all the wisdom of Egypt (1 Kings 4:29-30). Such comparisons imply not only difference but similarity: the nations around recognized wisdom, although only in a limited way because they did not know the source. International interactions obviously took place, however. Perhaps a deeper consideration of these kinds of interactions might spur us on to connect with people around us today who do not know the source of wisdom. Perhaps talking about wisdom and the source of it will "take their breath away"—and give them a glimpse of the Lord Jesus, the One "greater than Solomon" (Matthew 12:42). I wonder if any Egyptians ever read Solomon's version of their wisdom teachings and had their eyes opened to the Lord.

This section begins with a call to hear (Proverbs **22:17-21**), similar to the father's calls in Proverbs 1 – 9. In this call the speaker and addressee are not identified, although the subsequent repetition of "my son" (23:15, 19, 26; 24:21) implies a setting similar to the earlier instructions. The style of this section also recalls those opening chapters, with a number of proverbs flowing like paragraphs rather than standing independently in a series of discrete sayings.

Waltke helpfully crystallizes the symmetrical structure that we immediately sense in this introductory call of **22:17-21** (*The Book of Proverbs Chapters 15 – 31*, page 221). He sees the center, **verse 19**, as a "janus" (that is, a verse that looks both ways): back to a focus on the son (**v 17-18**) and ahead to a focus on the father who is speaking (**v 20-21**). They meet in the center—where the focus is on what? On the Lord. The center verse of the introduction stands out and holds out the point of all these sayings: "that your trust may be in the LORD" (**v 19a**).

We find again an insistent connection between hearing with the ear and applying in the heart:

"Incline your ear, and hear the words of the wise,
    and apply your heart to my knowledge." (**v 17**)

The next verse shows the continuation of the process, this time from inside out: these words will be pleasant, first, if kept deep within (literally "in your stomach"; see Tremper Longman, *Proverbs*, page 415), and then, second, if they are "ready on your lips" (**v 18**).

What a remarkably condensed and beautiful description of learning wisdom—with the end result "that you may give a true answer to those who sent you" (**v 21b**). It's not clear who *sent* this son (perhaps family or leaders grooming him for leadership), but the picture of him as a commissioned messenger fits well with the importance that Proverbs places on messengers (see 13:17; 25:13). It also fits well with the broader reach of Proverbs' wisdom to communicate truth. Today, we "messengers" of the gospel must be always prepared to give a reason for the hope that is in us (1 Peter 3:15).

The "thirty sayings" mentioned in Proverbs **22:20** reflect the influence of the Egyptian source, which has thirty chapters. The thirty sayings in this section are discernible (although different commentators divide them in slightly differing ways); we will examine the passages without numbering them.

Wise Interactions Part 1

After the opening call comes a section of varied proverbs that send the son (and us) out into the world to interact wisely with all kinds of people—especially the rich and poor. **Verses 22-23** immediately command justice for the poor. Oppression of the poor was the final concern of the previous collection (**v 16**), and here it is opening this next one.

But we need to look ahead as well. What most recognize as the first ten sayings in this collection begins and ends with defense of the poor and vulnerable: **v 22-23** and **23:10-11** give matching commands and reasons; they are like bookends. First, do not rob the poor or crush the afflicted at the gate (**22:22**), because "the LORD will plead their cause" (**v 23**). And then in **23:10**, do not "move an ancient landmark" (probably to take land from the poor) or "enter the fields of the fatherless" (probably to steal from the vulnerable)—for exactly the same reason:

"... for their Redeemer is strong;

he will plead their cause against you." (**v 11**)

With regard to the identity of the "Redeemer" in this context, we might think first of the provision of the Old Testament law for a redeemer in the form of a near kinsman who would provide for his relative's widow (Leviticus 25:25; Ruth 3:12-13). But this word is used many times in the Old Testament for God himself—as is surely the case here, especially in light of Proverbs **22:23**.

Many of these examples relate to matters of civic justice: "the gate" in **verse 22** would be the entrance to a city where elders decided matters of justice; it was their courtroom. The "ancient landmarks" (**23:10**; see **22:28**) were not just tradition; they marked God's sovereign distribution of the promised land to the tribes of Israel, as recorded in the law (Deuteronomy 19:14; 27:17). These proverbs address not just private oppression but also the political sorts of corruption that enable it, especially when those with power rule selfishly over those with none.

> God cares for and will defend the poor and vulnerable—and to be wise is to be like him in this regard.

Gates and ancient landmarks don't directly apply to us today. What does apply is God's clear message that he cares for and will defend the poor and vulnerable—and that to be wise is to be like him in this regard. In these proverbs the Lord is not pictured as standing back and responding to this or that; he is active, proactive, stepping forward to "plead the cause" of the defenseless and punish those who harm them.

Our particular contexts will guide what this needs to mean for us. But these proverbs should certainly challenge each of us, whatever our contexts, to be like our Father, who did not let us die, even when we were helpless and hopeless and deserving death, but who sent his own Son to save us.

Who are the poor or defenseless near you, whose cause you could plead and whose lives you might help light up with God's justice and God's mercy, ultimately shown in Christ? Who are your needy neighbors just a few streets away? One unavoidable subject in this regard is surely abortion. A pregnant woman is vulnerable, and the baby in her womb is utterly defenseless. We cannot escape being complicit in this issue that connects to the people and the power of the societies and the communities in which we live. Consider these related and convicting verses from later in this section:

"Rescue those who are being taken away to death;
   hold back those who are stumbling to the slaughter.
If you say, 'Behold, we did not know this,'
   does not he who weighs the heart perceive it?
Does not he who keeps watch over your soul know it,
   and will he not repay man according to his work?"

(Proverbs **24:11-12**)

Wise Interactions Part 2

Continuing to observe this first group of sayings, we find three subsections in the middle that also relate to wealth and poverty—this time in more private settings. In two of them we're invited to dinner (**23:1-3** and **v 6-8**). The first meal is hosted by someone rich and important—a "ruler" (**v 1**)—and the second by someone rich but mean—a "stingy" man (**v 6**). Both men serve "delicacies" which the son is told not to desire (**v 3, 6**).

In both scenes, the son is called to restrain his appetite and to see through deception to discern the truth. The ruler's "deceptive food" (**v 3**) is perhaps to test or obligate him in some way, or maybe he's simply being warned that the delicacies of wealth can themselves become an entrapment—such a serious one that he should put a knife to his throat if he is "given to appetite" (**v 2**).

It's possible that **22:29** leads into this scene: the guest might be the one who is "skillful in his work" and gets invited to visit kings. To be skillful in work is valuable and good; indeed it is part of wisdom. But wisdom must invade all the categories of our lives—including our physical appetites and our appetites for wealth and prestige.

The stingy man's deception is his hypocrisy: he seems hospitable, with his hearty-sounding invitations to eat and drink, but "his heart is not with you" (**23:7**). The son will later "vomit up the morsels" he's eaten, realizing the deception and the waste of his pleasant words on an evil man (**v 8**). **Verse 9** may be taken as part of this sub-section, as it advises, "Do not speak in the hearing of a fool," who will despise words of good sense.

In between these two dinner scenes comes the lesson to be learned: wisdom's discernment in matters of wealth. It's a lovely passage:

"Do not toil to acquire wealth;
   be discerning enough to desist.
When your eyes light on it, it is gone,
   for suddenly it sprouts wings,
flying like an eagle toward heaven." (**v 4-5**)

Although wealth is often the reward of the wise in Proverbs, it is never a prize to be grasped for or toiled for. The memorable image of these verses shows the folly of such misplaced desire—as wealth sprouts wings and flies away like an eagle. These passages are about our heart's desire, which can so easily be captured by things that will pass away.

Other interactions appear in this section: there's the angry man we noted in introducing synonymous parallelism (**22:24**). We've seen how the lines of this verse repeat but also progress, suggesting a growing danger. **Verse 25** actually continues the statement and articulates the danger, although perhaps not the danger we would have thought of first. We might have first feared being hurt by the angry person. But the danger first stated is that we might learn to *act* like that wrathful person, and we will become "entangled ... in a snare." It would be a hurtful snare indeed, of strife and broken relationships—the kind of snare we know well in a broken world. This section of proverbs reveals a world full of interactions that need a heart desiring wisdom—a heart that trusts in the Lord (**22:19**).

Questions for reflection

1. In a world of people searching for wisdom, how might Proverbs equip you to share wisdom, which is ultimately revealed to us in Christ?

2. In what ways does God's heart for the poor and vulnerable bless and challenge you?

3. What are some differences between working hard to make a living and toiling to acquire wealth?

PART TWO

A Matter of the Heart

Proverbs **23:12** begins another call to wisdom, using the always-related words "instruction" and "knowledge." The focus here is on the heart: the father pours out his heart and pleads for the heart of his son:

"Apply your heart to instruction
    and your ear to words of knowledge." (**v 12**)

"My son, if your heart is wise,
    my heart too will be glad." (**v 15**)

"Let not your heart envy sinners,
    but continue in the fear of the LORD all the day." (**v 17**)

It's notable that two verses advocating discipline come in the middle of these warm, affectionate verses in which the father obviously yearns for the good of his child. Only in this loving context does discipline find its proper place. **Verses 13-14** urge discipline, and even the striking of a child with a rod—which will not kill him but might "save his soul from Sheol." As noted earlier in connection with 22:15 (see also 13:24 and 19:18), whatever specific stance we might take on corporal discipline, the clear principle is that children need discipline—both instruction in good ways and consequences for bad ways.

The consistent assumption is that we live in a fallen world, with folly bound up in the heart of each one of us (see 22:15). Only as we learn to fear the Lord and listen to his word are we enabled to turn from the path of death to the path of life. Proverbs virtually shouts the importance of teaching God's word to young people so that they can hear early and "direct their hearts" in the way of wisdom (**23:19**).

Of course, such views are utterly contrary to many of the assumptions around us today: that children are by nature good; that they should be allowed to find their own way according to their natural desires; that rules and discipline constrict rather than enable; that human civilization is progressing in its understanding of human behavior, gradually discarding old and harmful ideas to embrace new and freeing ones. We might tend to feel threatened by the onslaught of such ideas. Proverbs tells us to see them for what they are: foolish and contrary to the word of God, which must remain our confidence and our strength along the path that truly does lead to life.

It is worth repeating that the context for discipline is that of love (see 3:11-12). Those verses from Proverbs 3 are directly quoted in Hebrews 12:5-6, where the writer to the Hebrews calls believers to consider the suffering that Christ endured for us, so that we might not grow weary or fainthearted—under the Lord's disciplining hand. "It is for discipline that you have to endure. God is treating you as sons," Hebrews 12:7 tells us. "For the moment all discipline seems painful rather than pleasant, but later it yields the peaceful fruit of righteousness to those who have been trained by it" (Hebrews 12:11).

The father's call here in Proverbs is a call of love—and a call of hope. Building on the admonition to continue in the fear of the Lord (Proverbs **23:17**), **verse 18** makes a large affirmation, looking ahead into a future that is undefined but sure:

"Surely there is a future,
    and your hope will not be cut off."

Heartfelt Relationships

Proverbs' hope is not offered as an abstract proposition. It comes in the context of relationships—first with the Lord whom we fear, and also with the family who passes on the word. If you are the first in your family line to know the Lord—that is, if you did not have the joy of receiving godly instruction from parents or family—then you can adopt Proverbs' perspective of hope: you can pass it on to others after you. Whoever instructed you is your family in the Lord, and whatever kind of family the Lord gives you is a huge channel of instruction that you are called to carry on.

Verses 22-25 highlight the specific relationship of the son to his parents, who are instructing him. It's not just that they say he must listen to them; it's also a call to recognize and respect the deep nature of the relationship of children to their parents. It's the call of the fifth commandment: to "honor" your father and your mother (Exodus 20:12). It's not just because they're wise; it's that your father "gave you life" (Proverbs **23:22**) and your mother "bore you" (**v 25**). And it's not just to obey the commandment; it's also so that your parents will "greatly rejoice" and be "glad" in their child (**v 24-25**; see 10:1).

This is beautiful. And this is hard for children to do, because folly is so bound up in all our hearts. The force of this call through the book makes clear the force of sin's pull to disobey. **23:22** includes a haunting second line—one suggesting that our tendency to disobey the fifth commandment persists into adulthood: "And do not despise your mother when she is old." The implication is that along with gaining years, she has gained wisdom—so keep listening to her. The implication is also that there exists a temptation to "despise" (scorn, or at least stop honoring) aged parents. Elderly parents are increasingly slow and weak; it takes effort for adult children to make their parents a part of their lives. Energetic grandchildren and great-grandchildren have to be taught to stop and converse with them thoughtfully, by phone or video call—and even more face to face, when the swirl of action and quick conversation can too often leave the elderly behind. There is a lot to think on and work on here.

"My son, give me your heart," says the father, and "observe my ways": follow my example (**v 26**). For a father to be able to say this, he must be living a faithful life before his children—and repenting when he sins (which he will). In this context comes another warning against the prostitute or the adulteress: "like a robber" along the path she "lies in wait" to capture people and turn them from good to evil (**v 27-28**). This figure, again, shows both the specific evil of sexual temptation and also the potent danger of evil—evil that doesn't just happen to us but that targets us and takes us down, as the serpent did to Eve in the Garden of Eden. Hence the need for warning, instruction, and discipline, lovingly passed down from generation to generation of those who fear the Lord.

Misguided Hearts: From Gluttons to Drunkards

The two evils most specifically targeted by the father in these passages are gluttony and drunkenness—sins that often go together and that are put together, twice, in **verses 20-21**. The father has just told his son to direct his heart in the way of wisdom (**v 19**); **verse 20** then warns about the *other* way, on which are found gluttons and drunkards. We often scold about drunkenness while forgetting to note the evil of gluttony, which equally represents a lack of restraint and an improper desire; so, in these verses, the dire consequences of poverty and rags are applied to both together.

To warn of drunkenness, this section includes a remarkable passage (**v 29-35**) that doesn't just argue the evil of too much alcohol; it takes us into the very experience of drunkenness. It dizzies us, perhaps makes us laugh (momentarily), and thoroughly impresses us with the deadly dangers of drunkenness.

> We often scold about drunkenness while forgetting to note the evil of gluttony, which equally represents a lack of restraint and an improper desire.

In **verse 29**, six questions play a "Guess Who" game with the reader, sketching a portrait of a woefully sad, quarrelsome, sullen, bruised, red-eyed person. Who is it? **Verse 30** answers: "those who tarry long over wine." Not only have they drunk too much, but they've given a lot of time to it. Alcohol is a big part of their life and pleasure—as evidenced in the command of **verse 31**: not just not to drink too much but not to "look at" the wine, at the way it sparkles red and "goes down smoothly." Implied is a kind of abandonment of oneself to the sensual pleasure, which is very different from enjoying alcohol with restraint.

Proverbs is not speaking to whether or when we should consume alcohol. Described here is the destructive folly of overconsumption. **Verse 32** makes the warning clear, picturing this sparkling pleasure as in the end being like a deadly snake: it "bites like a serpent" and "stings like an adder." The warning is elaborated with more imagery in **verses 33-35**, capturing the disorientation of an inebriated person. **Verse 33** describes blurry vision or even a hallucination, and uncontrolled words from the heart: words that are not only slurred but "perverse." **Verse 34** offers an intriguing picture:

"You will be like one who lies down in the midst of the sea,

like one who lies on the top of a mast."

We're to imagine this swaying person who desperately needs to find a place to lie down but collapses in the most life-threatening spots conceivable: on the ocean waves or high on top of a ship's mast. Both images could make you seasick (maybe that's part of the point). The point also is the unreasonable and self-destructive nature of these impulses; we picture this figure sinking into the sea or plunging to his death. The final point: there is no place of rest for this person.

Verse 35 is a sad one, in which we hear the voice of the drinker telling how he was struck and beaten but couldn't feel anything; his senses have been numbed. He's lost his senses; all he can say is:

"When shall I awake?

I must have another drink."

Proverbs takes time to develop this portrait; we should take time to ponder it. We all surely know some or many whose lives have been destroyed by the deadly effects of alcohol or drugs or whatever people find to jumble their senses repeatedly until they've lost them. These dangers are not new. From generation to generation, people with godly sense must pass on these warnings, embedding them in loving instruction that turns hearts toward knowing and fearing the Lord.

The first couple verses of chapter 24 may conclude this whole section that began in **23:12** with a focus on the heart. The counsel in **24:1** is not to envy evil men or desire to be with them. Why? **Verse 2** tells us that "their hearts devise violence"—violence that comes out on their lips. Their hearts and their words reveal the opposite of the fear of the Lord, as we've seen in the examples of gluttony and drunkenness.

But these verses also serve to introduce the next section, which concludes the "Words of the Wise."

Wisdom Versus Folly

The final section of the "Words of the Wise" exalts wisdom's goodness and strength. **Verses 1-2** and **verses 19-22** work as a pair of bookends: both units call the listener not to envy the wicked or to desire to join them. Their evil lives contrast with the life of wisdom that this section describes, and the final verses describe an end that contrasts finally with the hope given to those who fear the Lord.

Within the bookends of these calls not to envy or join evildoers comes this section's climactic call to follow wisdom (as opposed to folly). **Verses 3-4** take us back to Proverbs 9, with Wisdom building her house, preparing her feast, and calling us in. Note the cluster of weighty wisdom words in this rich picture of wisdom's house:

"By wisdom a house is built,
     and by understanding it is established;
   by knowledge the rooms are filled
     with all precious and pleasant riches." (**24:3-4**)

The picture of wisdom's house has consistently shown us a network of relationships—first with the Lord himself, as wisdom in action points to his grace and provision. This house is a picture not only of where we should live but of where we should most want to live—in the Lord's presence. *In contrast to envying the wicked,* Proverbs is saying, *this is what your heart should seek.* **Verses 13-14** picture the sweet dripping of the honeycomb: "Wisdom is such to your soul" (**v 14a**).

It's a good test of our souls: to ask what we really desire, deep down. Where do our thoughts go when we wake up in the middle of the night, or when we first wake up in the morning? What kind of desire motivates us to exercise and diet—what are we after? Do we hunger for God's word? Does it fill our minds regularly? Proverbs helps us desire this wisdom of God that so infuses all of life; it makes us want to live in wisdom's house. Proverbs helps us seek after the Lord Jesus, who is our wisdom from God.

The passage goes on to describe "a wise man"; he lives in that house and reflects its stability and goodness. Emphasized here is the wise man's "strength" and "might" (**v 5**), referring not to his muscles but to his wisdom, and the wisdom of many through whose guidance wars are waged and victory is won (**v 6**).

Verse 7's final comment here about wisdom is that it is "too high for a fool"; he isn't even capable of joining the conversation "in the gate," where the wise leaders gather. This verse makes a transition from the wise to fools and evildoers—perhaps the very ones against whom the wise wage war and win (**v 7-9**). The worst sinner, the scoffer, this time is called an abomination not to the Lord but "to mankind" (**v 9**). This passage calls out the wise to see evil for what it is, never to envy it, and always to stand up against it—as in **verses 10-12**.

We noted **verses 11-12** earlier, in the context of defending the poor and defenseless. In this chapter celebrating the strength of the wise, **verse 10** seems to call out those of us who "faint in the day of adversity," showing that our strength is small. This verse surely refers to the strength of heart that wisdom brings. Proverbs is telling us where to look for that strength: to the Lord whom we fear. "A wise man is full of strength" (**v 5a**).

Followers of the Lord get to live in that house full of knowledge and understanding, from which we can emerge fully equipped for the "day of adversity" (**v 10**). There will indeed be days of adversity. But, as verse 16 says, "The righteous falls seven times and rises again." The wicked will stumble and fall (**v 16-17**), but the righteous are pictured as falling and *rising*, again and again—never defeated.

Amid talk of war and victory and strength and the wicked falling, **verses 17-18** stop us short if we are those who have a tendency to gloat over the fall of our enemies. Scripture shows plenty of righteous rejoicing in God's victories over his enemies, but this prohibited rejoicing is a gladness of heart at our enemy's fall—seemingly from a more personal sense of self-righteous revenge—which displeases God when he sees it, so much that he may turn his anger away from our enemy.

Only with a humble heart that fears the Lord can we affirm the ultimate difference between the wise and the foolish: one has hope, and one does not. Contrast these two very clear verses:

"If you find it [wisdom], there will be a future,
and your hope will not be cut off." (**v 14**)

"… for the evil man has no future;
the lamp of the wicked will be put out." (**v 20**)

This hope is only in the Lord. The final command of the "Words of the Wise" is to "fear the LORD and the king" (**v 21a**). As we have seen, these two are not equal, but they are connected; the kings of Israel were established to show the Lord's perfectly righteous and just rule. The broader, related principle is that of respecting any governing authority because it is placed there by God's sovereign hand (Romans 13:1-7).

How wonderful to find that the wisdom borrowed and adapted from Egyptian writings turns us in the end back to the beginning: to the fear of the Lord. This is the word of the Lord, from his mouth.

"More Sayings of the Wise"

The rest of Proverbs 24 consists of added but consistent sayings—almost like a postscript to the words we have just examined. Its topics can be summed up with two words that cover our daily lives in a comprehensive way: words and work.

First, words—a topic we've seen before and will see again. Here, the context seems to be something like a trial or court setting, with judging (**v 23**) and witnesses (**v 28**). **Verses 23-26** make the point that words must address people or situations honestly, without partiality, for "partiality in judging is not good" (**v 23b**). Calling the wicked "right" will bring cursing from peoples and nations (**v 24**); on the other hand, rebuking the wicked will bring delight and blessing (**v 25**). **Verse 26** expresses the delight and blessing of honest words, comparing them to a (delightful!) kiss.

This principle of honest judgment and speech applies anywhere, but the need for it in legal and political dealings always has been great, and still is today. Rhetoric in such contexts is often riddled with partiality to one agenda or another. A figure who speaks out publicly with straightforward honesty stands out. Those who follow the Lord Jesus must aim to encourage and support such honest people (for they will face adversity), as well as, by God's grace, being those honest people.

Likewise, **verses 28-29** speak to those called to serve as a witness, possibly in the trial of a neighbor. Any personal agenda is again forbidden; if the neighbor has wronged us, we cannot seize the opportunity to exact revenge through deceitful words. As God's word is truth, so must our words be.

The chapter closes by coming home to our workaday world. **Verse 27** offers sensible prudence that is especially helpful for young people in the beginning stages of career or marriage. The point of preparing the fields outside before building a house is to recommend diligence and wise priorities in planning, instead of jumping in without looking ahead.

Finally, the sluggard—here he is one more time (still not the last!). The closing verses (**v 30-34**) are like a little fable, with a lesson. After the speaker describes walking by the sluggard's vineyard and seeing it uncared for and unprotected, overgrown with thorns and nettles, he says:

"Then I saw and considered it;
    I looked and received instruction." (**v 32**)

The lesson concerns the folly of lazy procrastination, and also the wisdom of receiving instruction along wisdom's path. Proverbs helps us *see*, and *consider*, and *receive instruction*—all with a humble heart, as we learn to walk in the fear of the Lord.

Questions for reflection

1. How does Proverbs challenge or encourage you on the subject of discipline?

2. How do you respond to Proverbs' passages on gluttony and drunkenness? What do these issues have to do with our hearts for the Lord?

3. Proverbs is ultimately a hopeful book. What passages from this part of Proverbs have lifted your heart to hope—and lifted your heart to Jesus?

11. SOLOMON REPRISE

Proverbs **25:1** introduces chapters 25 – 29: "These also are the proverbs of Solomon which the men of Hezekiah king of Judah copied." King Hezekiah ruled from 715-687 BC, over 200 years after King Solomon. During his reign Hezekiah restored temple worship according to the law (see 2 Kings 18 – 20; 2 Chronicles 29 – 32), and he apparently supervised the formation of this added collection of Solomon's proverbs. We'll look at chapter 25 in some detail, and then chapters 26 – 29 a bit more generally. These chapters offer wisdom that is less intimate than in the father-son exchanges, and that is more public, as to a group in leadership training.

Humble Before Kings

We're clearly in a courtly setting in this opening section, with kings (**25:1-6**), "the great" (**v 6**), a noble (**v 7**), a court (presumably the king's, **v 8**), and a ruler (**v 15**). It makes sense to take these proverbs as addressing someone who needs to learn how to get along in noble society. And the quality he needs is humility.

First and foremost, humility is needed before the glory of God and kings. God and kings are again linked; they were linked earlier in sovereign judgment, and here they are linked in "glory" (**v 2**). Their glories, however, differ; God's glory is "to conceal things," whereas the glory of kings is "to search things out." God's glory is clearly superior in that all mysteries are hidden in his sovereign majesty; kings are glorious in their God-granted privilege of searching out these mysteries (as Solomon in his wisdom did).

Why do we find the more general name "God" (*Elohim*) here, as opposed to the name "LORD" (*Yahweh*) which has been used regularly in Proverbs to refer to the covenant God of Israel? Waltke explains that the passage points to the **transcendent** God of creation, whose mysteries are expressed in verse 3 as the heights of the heavens and the depths of the earth (*The Book of Proverbs Chapters 15 – 31*, page 311). These creational mysteries, however, are used to picture the unsearchable heart not of God but of kings. Why? Perhaps because the listener is to learn that he can no more understand a king's heart than he can understand the greatest mysteries of God's creation. From God's perspective the king's heart is not unsearchable; it's a stream of water in his hand (21:1). But from the perspective of one who should humbly fear the Lord and the king (24:21a), one glory reflects the other.

25:4-5 calls for humility through the picture of a silversmith removing impurities from silver in order to make a vessel. The point is that the wicked must be removed from the king's presence, so that "his throne will be established in righteousness" (**v 5**). The one in training must humbly ask, *Am I righteous and worthy to serve the king? Am I zealous for righteousness to fill the king's court, and for wickedness to be expelled?*

Let's step back for a moment. We have acknowledged the difficulty of applying "kingly wisdom" today, as we struggle to find glory and righteousness shining through any ruler. Was it easier in the time of David and his descendants? Surely not. The Israelites held on to the promise of a righteous, eternal ruler in the line of David, but David himself and all the kings after him sinned in the Lord's sight, some grievously and unrepentantly. To take away all the wicked from the king's presence might take away the king as well. Hezekiah's men who were copying these proverbs knew how the kingdom had been divided and permeated by sin, from the top down.

But Proverbs always lets us see through the king to the Lord. Everything depends not on the king but on the glorious God who promised a perfect king. The prophet Isaiah spoke of that king:

"Of the increase of his government and of peace
> there will be no end,
on the throne of David and over his kingdom,
> *to establish it and to uphold it*
with justice and with righteousness
> from this time forth and forevermore.
The zeal of the LORD of hosts will do this."

> (Isaiah 9:7, my emphasis; see Proverbs **25:5b**; 29:14)

Proverbs' lessons of humility before kings make sense ultimately because of this promised King. He came; he showed us humility as he took on himself the form of a servant and died for us; he rose from the grave; and he ascended into heaven—our glorious, risen King who will come back to judge all and to reign with his people in perfect justice and righteousness forever. Those who serve him are in training for the court—the worldwide court of the true King.

More Lessons in Humility

Some of these lessons in humility actually sound a lot like ones taught by King Jesus himself while he was here on earth. **25:6-7** sounds familiar because Jesus taught basically the same lesson (Luke 14:7-11). Proverbs' point is this: don't "put yourself forward in the king's presence"; it is better to be called up from the back than to be sent back from the front (**v 6-7**). Jesus' parable was set not at court but at a wedding feast; the point, however, was the same: "Everyone who exalts himself will be humbled, and he who humbles himself will be exalted" (Luke 14:11).

To be "put lower" publicly, especially before a "noble" (Proverbs **25:7b**), would bring shame. That word "shame" appears twice in **verses 8-10**, which advise humility in dealing with a neighbor—not rushing to make public a complaint against your neighbor, in case you yourself might be put publicly to shame. Many from non-Western cultures who base their thoughts and actions more on communal shame and honor than we in the West tend to do would grasp more acutely the weight of shame and the blessing of honor dealt with here. Proverbs' call is to avoid shame not by self-exaltation or self-abasement but by humility—being honest first about your own failings, and then honest with others about theirs. This actually sounds a lot like needing to take the log out of your own eye before being able to see clearly enough to take out the speck in your brother's eye (Luke 6:41-42).

> Proverbs' call is to avoid shame not by self-exaltation or self-abasement but by humility.

Next are two pairs of proverbs that teach humility in the way we speak and listen. Proverbs **25:11** is often quoted; it offers an exquisite picture for words that are "fitly spoken"—true and beautiful words, offered from a wise heart to the right person at the right time in the right place:

"A word fitly spoken
   is like apples of gold in a setting of silver."

Surely the following verse, with its co-ordinating gold jewelry, relates. The "word fitly spoken" may be **verse 12**'s reproof given by a "wise reprover" and received by a humble listener; the beauty here is like a gold ring or an ornament of gold. The words of wisdom themselves are exquisitely beautiful; passed on and humbly received, they become beauty that you can wear like the finest jewelry, everywhere you go. The one instructed here is being encouraged to listen to reproof and to be adorned by wisdom.

Recently in my church Bible-study small group, as we were discussing the first verses of James, about counting it joy when we meet **trials**, one of the younger women expressed frustration at the difficulty of believing these verses and actually putting them into practice. One of the older women, who doesn't talk a lot, spoke up at that point and gently explained to this younger woman how she had learned the truth of those verses by persevering through many years of hardship—and how she had gradually, truly come to know joy in her Savior. As she spoke, her face was full of joy and a kind of beauty that is way better than no wrinkles and creases. And as she spoke, I saw that joy received and reflected in the younger woman's face. It was a moment of gold, and the kind of moment of which Proverbs is speaking here.

Verses 13-14 compare two kinds of words: those of a faithful messenger who brings a true report and those of a boaster who makes false promises. Connecting the two contrasting proverbs are images from nature: the messenger is like the cold of snow refreshing the workers sweating in the fields at harvest time; the boaster is "like clouds and wind without rain," promising gifts that never materialize. The more unusual third line in **verse 13** ("he refreshes the soul of his masters") highlights the good of a faithful messenger and sets a worthy aspiration for anyone serving another. It should prompt us to ask ourselves, "Would those with whom I live and work say that I refresh their souls?"

The final proverb in this explicitly courtly section continues the focus on words, advocating "patience" and a "soft" tongue, which are powerful enough to persuade a ruler and "break a bone" (**v 15**). It takes humility to wait and to listen, rather than to speak or act hastily or demandingly. This entire first section is calling for humble restraint that honors others—and God first, the glorious One who created and rules us all.

Humble Restraint in an Unrestrained World

The rest of chapter 25 brings a remarkable array of images that drive home the proverbs' points. We're no longer in the king's court. The majority of **verses 16-28** describe wicked or at least problematic people who are certainly not acting in the way recommended for the court. And wisdom calls for the same humble restraint here as previously.

In the middle of these proverbs come two verses that stand out not only for their mention of the Lord but also for their summation of a wise person's response to a world of evil:

"If your enemy is hungry, give him bread to eat,
    and if he is thirsty, give him water to drink,
for you will heap burning coals on his head,
    and the LORD will reward you." (**v 21-22**)

This is not only a call to restraint in taking vengeance on our enemies; more than that, it is a call to do good to them, giving bread and water—hopefully awakening their consciences, which will burn in them—and waiting on the Lord for justice. 20:22 told us not to repay evil, but to "wait for the LORD, and he will deliver you."

We might hear other echoes in our minds—for example, from Jesus' teaching: "Love your enemies, do good to those who hate you" (Luke 6:27) or from Peter's words describing the Lord Jesus who suffered for us: "When he was reviled, he did not revile in return; when he suffered, he did not threaten, but continued entrusting himself to him who judges justly" (1 Peter 2:23). Jesus came and showed us how to live out this wisdom, in the process of delivering us sinners who can't.

Surrounding this ray of light in the middle are verses that acknowledge how much we need this light. Some of the images are amusing; the tone is not heavy. But all the verses show a world muddied by sin—all except Proverbs **25:25**, which reminds us of **verse 13**:

"Like cold water to a thirsty soul,
    so is good news from a far country."

This verse stands out like the good news it talks about. We sense a longing here, in the midst of sin, for good news that will make things right. We also are being told that such good news comes.

In the meantime, we find pictures like that of eating too much honey and vomiting (**v 16**), which speaks for itself (and which accompanies **verse 17**, where your neighbor has too much of you). A man who bears false witness is like a whole pile-up of weapons (**v 18**). A treacherous man who breaks our trust just when we need him is like a "bad tooth" or a "foot that slips" (**v 19**). One who "sings songs to a heavy heart" (treating another's grief casually) is like the chill of undressing in the cold or the harmful effect of pouring vinegar on soda (**v 20**). A backbiting tongue and angry looks are like the north wind (**v 23**). And—in case we've forgotten—sharing a house with a quarrelsome wife is not *like* something; it's *worse*. Living in a corner of the roof is better (**v 24**).

The chapter's last three verses close with pictures that warn the listener not to give in to sin. **Verse 26** offers disturbing pictures and ominous words:

"Like a muddied spring or a polluted fountain
  is a righteous man who gives way before the wicked."

Those words "righteous" and "wicked" have not appeared since **verse 5**; nor has the word "glory," which we met in verse 2 and which now reappears in **verse 27**. As these final verses pull together the chapter, they remind us of the glorious king and the Lord God, in whose righteous presence we should humbly serve and on whom we should wait.

Verse 27 and **verse 28** both call for "self-control" as they picture what happens without it; it may not seem a great tragedy to eat too much honey (again) (**v 27**; see **v 16**), but the tragic truth is huge: without self-control, you're "like a city broken into and left without walls" (**v 28**).

Self-control is part of the humble restraint called for throughout this chapter. Don't put yourself forward. Don't rush to talk about others. Listen to reproof. Don't boast of more than what is true. Don't strike back at your enemy; serve him bread. This wisdom has a sound quite different from the voices around us calling us to follow our natural impulses, share our thoughts quickly for all the world to hear, and make platforms for ourselves on which we often boast a little too much—like the clouds and wind without rain.

Wait for the Lord, says Proverbs, *and he will deliver you* (20:22).

Questions for reflection

1. In what ways do you aim (or could you better aim) to "refresh the souls" of those with whom you live and work?

2. *Giving bread to your enemy…* what does that mean in your life? How does Jesus offer the ultimate example?

3. *Humble restraint…* what does (and doesn't) it mean? How did Jesus manifest this quality?

PART TWO

Focus on the Fool

Proverbs **26:1-16** presents the fool: to instruct the listener not to *be* him (of course), but also to show how to *deal with* him. The words "fool" and "folly" come a dozen times in **verses 1-12**; after that, the ultimate fool, the sluggard, takes over through to **verse 16**.

These verses instruct in dealing with fools—those who "despise wisdom and instruction" (1:7)—in two ways. First, *these verses instruct in what is fitting for a fool.* **26:1** makes it clear: "honor is not fitting for a fool," any more than snow fits summer or rain fits harvest time (see 19:10). "Fitting" according to what? As we've discussed, this book assumes a creational order instituted by God (which resonates with mention of the seasons), disrupted by sin, but still evident all around us and specifically revealed in God's word. Something "fitting" resonates with God's good order. Diligent work is fitting in God's good order. The marriage of a man and a woman is fitting. For a fool to receive honor is not fitting, for the fool does not honor the Lord. He is out of order. Giving honor to a fool is like fastening a stone inside a sling instead of slinging it out (**26:8**)!

What is fitting for fools? **Verse 3** answers: "a rod for his back"; in other words, punishment is fitting for him, for he refuses instruction or reproof. To disregard what fits a fool is to bring harm: to make him your messenger is like cutting off your own feet (**v 6**), and to hire a fool is to be like an archer who wounds everyone (**v 10**).

Second, *these verses instruct in how to talk (or not talk) to a fool—and, even more, how to understand (or not understand) these proverbs.* **Verses 4-5** are famous for their seeming contradiction:

"Answer not a fool according to his folly,
    lest you be like him yourself.
Answer a fool according to his folly,
    lest he be wise in his own eyes."

The principle of "fittingness" applies here as well: whether you follow the counsel of **verse 4** or **verse 5** depends on what fits the particular situation. In both verses the fool is spouting folly. But it takes wisdom to weigh the dangers: whether by answering you might be drawn yourself into the fool's spouting-off (**v 4**; see **29:9**), or whether by not answering you might encourage the fool to think he's spouting off wisdom (**26:5**). This verse implies there is a chance that this fool might be able to see his folly and turn from it; in that case it may be fitting to offer words that rebuke his folly.

These riddle-like instructions remind us of the way in which Proverbs itself has encouraged us to receive these wise sayings: not as rules or promises, but rather as wisdom that begins with the fear of the Lord and grows as we walk in relationship with him. It takes this foundation to discern and apply the proverbs' wisdom: to judge wisely, for example, whether **verse 4** or **verse 5** is fitting. "A proverb in the mouth of fools," says **verse 7**, is like a "lame man's legs," hanging useless—or it can even be harmful, like a thorn that hurts (**v 9**). Without the fear of the Lord, we cannot humbly receive these words with life-transforming understanding.

To round out this section on the fool, the sluggard makes his final appearance. Let's start with his final diagnosis, in **verse 16**:

"The sluggard is wiser in his own eyes
    than seven men who can answer sensibly."

Verse 5 first mentions the fool at risk of becoming "wise in his own eyes." Then **verse 12** tells us there is more hope for a fool than for one who is "wise in his own eyes." So, when we reach **verse 16**, we understand that a sluggard is worse than a fool—he is the most extreme example of folly.

To justify his inertia, he's still crying, "There is a lion in the road!" (**v 13**; see 22:13). **26:14**'s picture is wonderful: he's turning back and forth in his bed "as a door turns on its hinges"—not going anywhere, maybe just making irritating sounds. **Verse 15** shows him still stuck with his hand buried in the dish, too lazy to raise it to his mouth (see 19:24). The sluggard's folly might seem mostly harmless (or ridiculous). And yet here is a human being refusing to hear sense of any kind; he actually believes he's wiser than anyone. In this book of wisdom from God, that is the ultimate folly.

One final comment about the sluggard: we should take him both literally and not literally. We likely don't know any people with their hands stuck in bowls. But we do know people who think they're wise, who are stuck in life, and who are unwilling to get on with ordinary work that seems either too hard or too unsuited to what they consider their unique and highly developed gifts. We should all see the sluggard, consider, and receive instruction (24:32).

Folly's Words

The focus on the fool continues, with a particular focus on folly's words. **26:17-28** is violent and fiery, full of imagery that wakes us up to the power of words issuing from an evil heart. A quarrelsome person is like "one who takes a passing dog by the ears" (**v 17**—who would do that?), or like "charcoal to hot embers and wood to fire" (**v 21**). One who deceives and then says he was just joking (**v 19**—have you done that?) is "like a madman who throws firebrands, arrows, and death" (**v 18**). Whispers of gossip are like "delicious morsels," going down deep (**v 22**). These images throw open the shades even on casual or thoughtless words, letting us glimpse, through imaginary pictures, the real nature of what's happening.

Verses 23-26 get to the "heart" of the issue, contrasting gracious-sounding words with "an evil heart" (**v 23b**); a deceitful heart (**v 24b**); and a heart with "seven abominations" (**v 25b**)—seven symbolizing completeness, showing a heart "full up" with folly. **Verse 26** concludes with a solemn judgment of this deceiver:

"Though his hatred be covered with deception,
  his wickedness will be exposed in the assembly."

The Lord is not mentioned in this chapter. Our thoughts turn to him when we glimpse this picture of his people gathered, perhaps in a worship assembly, where the one with "fervent lips" and "evil heart" (**v 23**) is exposed. Even when the Lord is not named, especially by this point in the book we see his sovereign, ordering hand in the observation of **verse 27**, which paints a picture that "comes back on" all the evil-speakers in this section:

"Whoever digs a pit will fall into it,
    and a stone will come back on him who starts it rolling."

Swirls and Shepherds

Proverbs 27 (until the final five verses) offers one of the best examples of proverbs that swirl around us like the very swirl of life! We'll mention some of them, noticing in general that this chapter addresses various ordinary relationships with friends and neighbors and family, many of whom we've met before in Proverbs—including the quarrelsome wife, right there in the center (**27:15-16**). This is her final appearance. She's still like "a continual dripping on a rainy day" (**v 15a**), and it seems the dripping will never end, for to "restrain" her is like restraining the wind or grasping oil in your hand (**v 16**). It is terrible to hear of a husband essentially giving up on his wife. But it is profitable to see, consider, and receive instruction (24:32).

Proverbs 27 calls for humility amid the swirl. **27:1** tells us not to boast about tomorrow, "for you do not know what a day may bring" (see James 4:13-14). Proverbs **27:2** advises, "Let another praise you, and not your own mouth." Many of these proverbs reflect the blessing of unselfish friendship: "faithful are the wounds of a friend" (**v 6a**); the "sweetness" of a friend's "earnest counsel" makes the heart glad like oil and perfume (**v 9**). The well-known description of friendship as iron sharpening iron (**v 17**) implies not only a closeness but a willingness on the part of each to rebuke and to receive rebuke humbly.

The chapter's final section (**v 23-27**) offers a lyrical admonition to shepherds, telling them to watch carefully over their flocks, for from the lambs and goats come their livelihood, their clothing, and their sustenance. But another layer of meaning emerges in **verse 24**, which points out that riches will not last forever, and asks, "Does a crown endure to all generations?" Here a ruler—probably a king—is addressed and advised to watch carefully over his people, who are the lasting treasure.

Throughout the Old Testament, leaders of God's people are addressed as shepherds; the prophet Ezekiel was one of many who condemned the "shepherds of Israel" for abandoning their sheep (Ezekiel 34:1-10). In that prophecy the Lord says he will set over his people "one shepherd, my servant David ... he shall feed them and be their shepherd" (Ezekiel 34:23). In the line of David Jesus came, announcing, "I am the good shepherd" (John 10:11). King Jesus cares for his sheep indeed; he laid down his life for them.

Believers today do not look to kings to care for them. We look to the Lord who is our shepherd, even as David knew (Psalm 23:1). But we also look to those sometimes called "under-shepherds": pastors and elders who in the New Testament are called to shepherd their flocks with humble oversight (1 Peter 5:1-5). The people are the lasting treasure. "When the chief Shepherd appears," faithful under-shepherds will receive the "unfading crown of glory" (1 Peter 5:4). That crown does endure to all generations (see Proverbs **27:24**).

Remember the Two Ways

This final section (Proverbs 28 – 29) stands as a coherent unit, one that reminds us of the first part of Solomon's first collection. Antithetic parallelism makes a dramatic reappearance, re-establishing the pattern of contrasts that dominated Proverbs 10 – 15. Content is consistent with form: these chapters offer a final presentation of the two ways—that of wisdom traveled by the "righteous" and that of folly traveled by the "wicked."

Each proverb in Proverbs 28 – 29 bears pondering. And the pondering grows richer as more and more proverbs echo and connect with earlier ones. But these chapters also can be covered more summarily, as a conclusion to this section—which is what we will do here. Five observations will help illumine these concluding chapters.

1. These chapters are shaped by the contrast between the wicked and the righteous. With the return of antithetic parallelism as the dominant pattern, the tension between the two ways emerges repeatedly, and finds resolution. Five key verses stand out, articulate this tension, and provide structure for these two chapters:

■ **28:1** sets up the contrast between the wicked and the righteous, establishing from the start the greater strength and heart of the righteous, who are "bold as a lion."

■ **28:12** initiates a refrain that shows various kinds of rising and falling. Here, the triumph of the righteous in line 1 (with resulting glory) contrasts with the rising of the wicked in line 2 (with resulting fear). We're left wanting to hide, with the wicked rising.

■ **28:28** takes the second line of **verse 12** as its first line, with the wicked rising, but the second line by contrast pictures the wicked perishing and the righteous increasing. We're left with hope.

■ **29:2** takes the last phrase from the second line of **28:28** (with the righteous increasing) and shows the people rejoicing, but the second line by contrast shows the wicked ruling and the people groaning. We are left with dismay.

■ **29:16** is the last clear refrain, and it resolves the tension with finality. The first line shows the wicked increasing (with transgression increasing as well), but the second line asserts that "the righteous will look upon their downfall." We are left with hope—not yet complete resolution, as the downfall of the wicked is still in the undefined future. But we end with a picture of the righteous looking down upon the wicked, who have fallen. Indeed, "the righteous falls seven times and rises again," whereas the wicked stumble and fall (24:16).

These refrains give shape to the chapters; they also point in a larger way to the rise and fall of individuals and peoples and civilizations, as the battle between righteousness and evil persists. But these are not equal forces, with equal chances of rising, as these chapters clearly show.

2. These chapters emphasize the "law." Toward the beginning (**28:4, 7, 9**) and the end (**29:18**) we find mention of the law, which we have repeatedly seen as this book's crucial context. Proverbs' prologue (1:1-7) sets Proverbs in the context of the people of Israel—a people with a history as those chosen by God to receive and obey his word. They called the books of Moses the law (Hebrew *torah*); those five books also contained specific laws according to which the people were to live. The instruction mentioned in Proverbs can surely include wise teaching of various kinds, but Proverbs' prime emphasis throughout is on wisdom from God's mouth (2:6), given in God's inspired revelation—for Solomon's people, in the books of Moses. That revelation is now completed for us in the Old and New Testaments—including the instruction in this book of Proverbs.

We can take "law" here, then, to point to the word of God, and this understanding resonates with chapters 28 – 29. The three verses noted in chapter 28 make the law the foundation for understanding righteousness and wickedness, and worship. The parallelism of **29:18** makes "law" correspond to "prophetic vision": that is, to the special revelation of God's word to prophets (like Moses and those after him), who communicated that word to the people.

> We see a growing emphasis on justice, and on issues of wealth and poverty.

Growing up, I remember hearing this verse quoted in political contexts, as "Where there is no vision, the people perish" (KJV). The "vision" became whatever vision the speaker advocated, which illustrates the proverb's point: without revelation from God instructing us, we follow without restraint whatever direction we choose. This is Proverbs' point from the beginning: "Hear... Listen..." The words of wisdom to which we are called to listen are the very words of God.

3. These chapters emphasize justice. The law instructs in the ways of justice, especially for the poor and vulnerable. We see in Proverbs a growing emphasis on justice, and on issues of wealth and poverty; these themes continue to the end of this section, and are intimately connected with the overarching themes of righteousness and wickedness (see especially **28:3, 5, 8, 11, 16; 29:4, 7, 26**).

4. These chapters emphasize family and discipline. As we've seen, the context of parents and children is crucial in passing on wisdom from one generation to the next. In the midst of many proverbs here that show people's bent toward wickedness and their unrestrained evil (see, for example, **v 10, 11, 20**), we particularly notice God's provision for his children to be instructed and disciplined by human parents according to his word (see especially **28:7, 24; 29:3, 15, 17-19**).

5. These chapters turn us to the Lord. It is beautiful to trace the name of the Lord through these chapters, mentions of which are regularly spaced like stepping-stones, showing the way. The theme of justice, for example, connects with the word of the Lord and with the Lord himself; see especially **28:5, 25; 29:13**. An amazing mention of the Lord comes in **28:13-14**. Take time to study these two verses, find their gospel shape (see 16:5-6), and see once again the firm foundation of wisdom: the fear of the Lord.

The final few verses leave us with a focus on the Lord. Threatened with the rise of wickedness, we might fear (**29:25a**). But the parallel line reminds us that "whoever trusts in the LORD is safe." Threatened with injustice, we might put our faith in a ruler or political figure (**v 26**). But the parallel line reminds us that "it is from the LORD that a man gets justice." **Verse 27** closes the chapter with tension between the righteous and the wicked—but the Lord's justice in **verse 26** looms over the "unjust man" in **verse 27**.

Hezekiah's men must have felt like they were in school themselves as they copied these proverbs of Solomon. This collection sends us out to work and serve with humble restraint, aware of our need for wise discernment, and most of all with hearts of trust in the Lord and ears open to his word.

Questions for reflection

1. How would you explain Proverbs 26:4-5 to someone who's confused?

2. Are you aware of people "stuck in life," like the sluggard? What can you learn, and how can you help?

3. What are the gospel-shaped truths to be found and savored in Proverbs 28:13-14?

12. THE FEAR OF THE LORD: A PERSONAL GLIMPSE

Nobody knows who Agur is. He slips in and out of Scripture with the writing of Proverbs 30. But even in his strangeness Agur gives us the book's most personal account of what it's like to live out the fear of the Lord. We'll look at Agur's relationship with God (30:1-9), and then we'll hear his corresponding wise words about God's world (v 10-33). What we'll find, as we've found all along, is that wisdom does not exalt itself; a wise person receives God's gifts with a humble heart.

Who Is Agur?

Part of the problem in grasping Agur's identity is the difficulty of translating **verse 1**. Scholars differ (as evidenced in many Bible translations' footnotes) concerning the second part of this verse, in which Agur either declares his weariness or addresses some people whose names we do not recognize—or some combination of both.

There is agreement, however, on the introduction: "The words of Agur son of Jakeh," and significant consensus on the next words: "The oracle." Agur and Jakeh are both unknown; many guess that they were not Israelites. But the word "oracle," which also introduces the words of King Lemuel in 31:1, tells us that wherever Agur and Lemuel came from, the words that Scripture attributes to them are the word of the Lord. "Oracle" has the meaning the NIV gives it: "inspired utterance"—that is, words from God.

This is important, even as the connection to Egyptian texts was important earlier (22:17 – 24:22). God's sovereign inspiration of these words reached outside Israel's boundaries to bring in parts of this book. We don't know how it happened. Was Agur perhaps a **convert** to Judaism through interaction with Israel's wise men? It doesn't really matter how; it matters that we see God's sovereign hand over the world he created and loves—and, in Agur's case, over some person from somewhere with whom readers from all over everywhere can identify as he talks to us about his relationship with the Lord.

A Man Not Wise in His Own Eyes

Agur speaks from his heart. In **30:2-3**, he says things about himself that have led some to conclude he must be referring to a time before he knew the Lord:

"Surely I am too stupid to be a man.
    I have not the understanding of a man.
I have not learned wisdom,
    nor have I knowledge of the Holy One."

Why does Agur say he has not learned wisdom, and call himself stupid and without even human understanding? Consider what we might expect to hear at the end of a book about wisdom, especially from one aiming to help us "know wisdom and instruction," "understand words of insight," and so forth (1:1-7). We might expect someone at the end to step up and say, *I've got it. I have learned wisdom.*

On second thought, however, we might not expect that. We've just seen in chapter 26 the ultimate folly of being wise in one's own eyes (26:5, 12, 16). Proverbs has continually and increasingly connected the fear of the Lord with a humble and not an arrogant heart (see, for example, 15:33; 16:5-6; 21:4; 22:4; 29:23). The prologue called the wise to "hear and increase in learning" (1:5; see 9:9). A truly wise person would never stop, look at himself, and say he has learned wisdom.

What would the truly wise person say? Probably something like what Agur says in **30:2-3**. Longman advises us to take these verses as hyperbole, a figure of speech that uses exaggeration to make a point (*Proverbs*, page 521). That seems right. With as much literary force as possible, Agur is showing that he understands how small is his wisdom—how limited is his knowledge of the infinitely glorious "Holy One" (**v 3**; see 9:10).

Agur is not just looking at himself in a mirror or comparing himself with others; he is seeing himself (and all people) in light of the Holy One. His perspective shows in the questions he proceeds to ask:

"Who has ascended to heaven and come down?
    Who has gathered the wind in his fists?
Who has wrapped up the waters in a garment?
    Who has established all the ends of the earth?
What is his name, and what is his son's name?
    Surely you know!" (**30:4**)

What is the answer to these questions? The most obvious answer is "No one." No person has done any of these things; how, then, could any of us ever think we are wise? With the question about the names, Agur, in this wisdom context, demands the identity of this supremely wise person and that of his son, for that person has surely done what wise fathers do: they instruct their sons, passing on their wisdom to them. This would be one wise son to meet. The end is like a taunt: *Surely you know, all you who think you are wise!* But there is no such human father and son. That's the point.

Looking up to God, we find a different answer: "God." The resonances with Job are unmistakable here. Throughout Job 38, for example, the Lord questions Job in the same way that Agur is questioning those he addresses:

"Where were you when I laid the foundation of the earth?
    Tell me if you have understanding.
Who determined its measurements—surely you know!
    Or who stretched the line upon it?" (Job 38:4-5)

Job responds to the Lord:

"Behold, I am of small account; what shall I answer you?
   I lay my hand on my mouth." (40:4)

This sense of awe and reverence before the Lord God who created all things is at the heart of the wisdom that Proverbs (and all the Bible's wisdom literature) teaches.

Proverbs does not tell us the name of the son. We understand that the God of creation is being referenced—and we remember the claim of wisdom personified: "I was there" (Proverbs 8:27). But the question about this son hangs tantalizingly. Agur is calling for humility before God's mysteries.

Everything in us present-day Christians wants to shout that we know the son's name: Jesus! Looking back, we see the mystery solved. The author and theologian Graeme Goldsworthy suggests that in Jesus' conversation with Nicodemus in John 3, Jesus gives a direct answer to Agur's first question in Proverbs **30:4a** (*Proverbs: The Tree of Life*, Loc 2507 of 2736 in Kindle edition). Jesus explains, "No one has ascended into heaven except he who descended from heaven, the Son of Man" (John 3:13). Jesus was identifying himself as the answer to Agur's "Who?"—indeed, as the only man in whom all of heaven's wisdom is found.

Humility Before the Word

After setting our own small store of human wisdom in perspective, Agur celebrates the God who gives wisdom to us, in his word. He's affirming Proverbs' message from the beginning: "The Lord gives wisdom," and "from his mouth come knowledge and understanding" (Proverbs 2:6). And he's continuing the emphasis on *relationship* that we have seen throughout. Consider the two lines in **30:5**:

"Every word of God proves true;
   he is a shield to those who take refuge in him."

These are not two unrelated lines. They are actually a great corrective to any of us who might tend to isolate line 1 and simply wax eloquent on its theological truth. Indeed, not just Scripture's general meaning but Scripture's every word is true, written by authors who were carried along by the Holy Spirit to write down exactly the words God intended (2 Peter 1:21). But we must not stop there; it is through the perfectly true word of God that we know him and take refuge in him. The word "proves" in line 1 indicates a refining process: the truth of God's word is proven repeatedly; it shines out more and more brightly. Trusting this word is to take refuge in *him*; he *is* our shield (see 2:7). This is personal truth.

How interesting that the one thing he warns against, in relation to the word, is adding to it (**30:6a**). The risk is personal: God will rebuke you, and you will be found a liar (**v 6b**). But why is *adding* to God's word so emphasized? Deuteronomy 4:2 commands, "You shall not add to the word that I command you, nor take from it." Adding and taking away are both lying, and both bring God's wrath (see also Revelation 22:18-19).

Adding words to God's word is the height of arrogance. It's grasping for my voice to be heard, putting my wisdom on a level with God's. It's wanting more than what God has given. It's what the proud Pharisees in Jesus' time were doing, adding all their own rules and thereby "making void" God's word (see Mark 7:1-13). It's the attitude that the whole of Proverbs 30 warns against. It's what Agur will now ask God to protect him against, in his prayer.

Humility in Asking

Proverbs **30:7-9** is the only prayer in the entire book of Proverbs. It completes this chapter's first section, in which we are given a personal glimpse of someone who fears the Lord. What would such a person say about himself, or about God? This chapter has shown us. What would he say to God? We get to listen in here, not to a complete prayer but to the "asking" part—the part pertinent to the thrust of this chapter.

Most of us will have many things on our list of petitions to bring to God. Bible-study group members often put together prayer lists, and they can get long. And that's not bad. It's encouraging to be able to share our requests, and to know that brothers and sisters are praying—for our hearts, for loved ones, for challenges in health, finances, employment, and on and on.

But Agur has just two things on his list. These are the two things he'll pray until he dies (**v 7**). He's a minimalist; he's getting down to the basics here. These two things help all of us see through to the most basic concerns that should guide our petitions to the Lord. Agur uses the name *Yahweh*, the LORD, in **verse 9** of his prayer, showing that he knows not just God in general but the Lord of Israel: the One who mercifully reveals himself to his people.

The first request is this: "Remove far from me falsehood and lying" (**v 8a**). In the context of what we've just read (**v 5-6**), Agur is asking God to align his heart and his words with the truth of God's word: that he would not speak what God's word calls false; that he would not add to God's word; and that he would not listen to or promote false voices around him that go against God's word.

Implicit in this request is Agur's acknowledgment of his sin and weakness. He doesn't say, *Help me to believe and speak truth.* Rather, he asks God to remove falsehood, and to remove it not just from him but *far* from him; he knows his tendency to fall back into it. He evidences a humble and repentant heart before a holy God—as 28:13 describes:

"Whoever conceals his transgressions will not prosper,
    but he who confesses and forsakes them will obtain mercy."

Implicit also in this request is Agur's trust in God's word as having proven true, and in God as his shield and refuge from evil. He knows his weakness, but he also knows the Lord who will deliver him. And so he asks.

We could spend much time on this first request. Truthful words, and truth that resonates with God's word, might not be high on our list of requests—but maybe they should be. If at the end of each day we make it a practice to be quiet and simply think back through the words we have given out and taken in, we will have plenty to confess, and plenty to pray about.

Agur's second request comes in two parts—a two-pronged negative and a simple positive: first, "Give me neither poverty nor riches" (**30:8b**), and then, "Feed me with the food that is needful for me" (**v 8c**). **Verse 9** goes on to explain the risks he perceives in riches and poverty: risks relating not just to his own well-being but to his relationship with the Lord, and to the glory of the Lord's name. Agur is honest enough to admit to himself and before the Lord that he is vulnerable—as we all are, because of our sin. In wealth, he might come to feel self-sufficient and deny or simply forget about the Lord; in poverty, he might steal, and so "profane the name of my God."

> There is no virtuous economic situation *per se*; there is only the call to fear the Lord in the midst of whatever situation he ordains.

Proverbs has addressed the spectrum of economic situations and their complexities—the blessings and also the dangers of wealth, the plight of the poor, the goodness of integrity in the midst of little, and the need for generosity from those who have much. There is no virtuous economic situation *per se*; there is only the call to fear the Lord in the midst of whatever situation he ordains. When Agur asks for what is "needful," he seems to mean some point of moderation in between wealth and poverty. But he does not define that point. He is asking for whatever God knows he needs in order to walk according to God's word, glorifying his name. We can learn much from the deep humility in this request, as it ultimately trusts God to know better than we do what we need.

When Jesus taught his disciples to pray, "Give us this day our daily bread," he taught them to pray simply, like children who need care,

day by day. In my Bible, next to these two requests of Agur, I have written, "Clean me. Feed me." I don't remember if I heard someone say
that or if it's just what I noted about these two requests. It sums them
up pretty well—and that's humbling, because these two needs are the
two most basic needs of a little child. Maybe our prayers should go
back to such basics.

Questions for reflection

1. In what ways might people today be tempted to add to God's
   words?

2. What do you tend to ask God for, in regard to money? What do
   you learn from Agur's prayer?

3. Agur has a big view of God. What keeps us from such a view, and
   how can we increasingly share it?

PART TWO

Seeing Through Agur's Eyes

The first part of chapter 30 offers a uniquely personal glimpse into the humble heart of a wise man. The chapter's second part changes; it feels like Agur gets up from his prayers and goes outside. But it's still Agur, still with the same heart. In the rest of the chapter we observe the world through the eyes of a wise man with a humble heart.

A brief overview is helpful, as these verses can feel like random lists of various "things" coming at us that are not easy to hold together. First, let's notice three key points where a warning appears: **verse 10** begins the chapter's second half with a somewhat subtle warning; **verse 17** stops and gives a more dramatic warning; and **verses 32-33** conclude with a warning that clarifies (and vividly illustrates) the main point of the whole section.

These key points hold together various lists of observations. Between **verse 10** and **verse 17** come *two lists*:

- **Verses 11-14** list four arrogant kinds of people.

- **Verses 15-16** list first two, and then three—no, *four* things— that always want more.

Between **verse 17** and **verse 32** come *four lists*:

- **Verses 18-20** list first four wonderful things and then a terrible one.

- **Verses 21-23** list four over-reachers.

- **Verses 24-28** list four small wise things.

- **Verses 29-31** list four "stately" things.

Many of these verses are "numerical proverbs," listing a stated number of things that share a category. An early example appeared in 6:16-19—a list of seven things that are an abomination to the Lord. Often (not always) an introduction states the number of things to come, mentioning first the penultimate and then the final number (see **30:15, 18, 21, 29**). This method builds up expectation—perhaps for a list that could keep growing and growing, or perhaps in some cases for the final item as the climactic one in the list.

What is going on in all these lists? In general, they represent an ability to order and pattern reality, rather than simply to be buffeted by the swirl. The proverbs by nature do this kind of ordering: drawing comparisons; noting similarities and differences; distinguishing certain patterns of evil and righteousness and their consequences. This ability reflects the image of God our Creator, who in the beginning brought original order out of chaos—from the planets and stars all numbered and placed to the smallest living creatures in the sea and on the land.

Any time we make things with words whose meaning can be shared—from a grocery list to a poem—we reflect the image of God in us. We've seen the condensed nature of the poetic patterning in Proverbs, which is so effectively used to reflect and communicate the order that our Creator established in this world. As we fear the Lord and follow his word, we see more and more clearly into the patterns of God's order—and into the disorder brought by sin. Humble Agur's intensive organizing here at the end of Proverbs highlights this ability to see into God's order, to delight in the seeing, and to communicate what it means to live (and not to live) according to God's ways.

Proud Eyes

The warning that marks the beginning of this section cautions against slandering a servant to his master, for fear of being cursed by that servant and then held guilty (**30:10**). We've seen plenty of proverbs about the evil of slander, which uses false words to harm someone who is innocent. But the emphasis here seems to be on the set of relationships involved: to slander someone else's servant sounds like a pathetic attempt to raise oneself up by stepping on a person who is lowly and defenseless, and who works for someone else. The slanderer is stepping into a place that is not his, perhaps trying to expand his influence with some tempting secrets, and with a few words cruelly destroying the relationship of a servant with his master. No wonder that servant might curse you if you do this—and watch out: the defenseless might be defended after all, and you would be held guilty.

So begins a series of proverbs about the folly of self-exaltation and the wisdom of humility. The next set of four observations is not numbered; each is simply introduced with "There are those" (**v 11-14**). Each verse appears to describe a category of people who are exalting themselves in wrongful ways: children cursing the parents they should honor (**v 11**); filthy unwashed people who are "clean in their own eyes" (**v 12**); people who raise their eyes and look down on everybody (**v 13**); and, finally, those who violently wipe out the poor and needy from the earth (**v 14**). A summary doesn't capture the force of these verses, with their pictures of filthy excrement, eyelids rising high, teeth like swords, and fangs like knives, devouring the poor. Agur does not comment on these pictures; he just lays them out for us to see.

It's a violent, dark series of pictures, instructive for those of us today who sometimes look around and think the world must be worse than it has ever been before, with the breakdown of marriage and the family, poverty and injustice on all sides, the corruption of those in power, and on and on. It sounds like Agur understands. He has observed all this, named and categorized it, and passed it on so that we can learn from what he sees. It's a bigger story than just yours and mine. It's a more perennial problem than one that afflicts our culture in our time.

Verses 15-16 look into the natural world and find reflections of the quality we've seen in the previous verses: a grasping for more, a grasping that is never satisfied. Things that are non-human are personified, eerily communicating the pervasive effects of fallenness. First comes the leech, in two short and creepy lines that simply tell us, "The leech has two daughters," apparently named "Give and Give" (**v 15**). I've never closely observed a leech (a flat worm that attaches to flesh and sucks blood), but commentators are quick to note that the leech has two suckers, one protruding from each end: hence its two "daughters." The text gives no explanation--just the picture and the names. That's enough.

The leech is attached to another list, of four things that are explained, by the repeated words "never satisfied" and "never … enough" (**v 15-16**). The images piling up are deathly and disturbing: Sheol (the place of the dead), the barren womb, parched land, and fire. Deep within people and in all creation around us, ever since we were driven out of Eden, there is craving, craving, for what will fill (remember the soul-craving of the sluggard, 13:4).

Capping these lists of graspers-for-more is one of the chapter's "key points" in **30:17**, which stops and reaches back to verse 11 as it describes more dishonoring of parents by children—this time with a violent warning:

"The eye that mocks a father
   and scorns to obey a mother
will be picked out by the ravens of the valley
   and eaten by the vultures." (**v 17**)

> Huge trajectories can be set by just one moment when parents might be too busy to instruct or discipline.

The mocking child here is arrogantly scorning the good pattern repeatedly celebrated in this book, elevating himself over the ones to whom he should humbly look and listen. After the lists we've seen so far, scorning a parent may seem an anti-climactic evil to receive such a climactic warning. And yet in that one scene of a child's mocking are the seeds of full-blown evil. Huge trajectories can be set by just one moment, or two or three, when parents might be too busy to instruct or discipline their child—or one moment, or two or three, when a child gives that "eye" to Mom or Dad. With rejection of the good pattern of children honoring parents comes implicit rejection of the divine authority that the pattern reflects.

We can't overlook that mocking "eye" (**v 17**), especially after reading about those haughty eyes in **verses 12-13**. Is there an echo here of the ultimate folly of being wise in your own eyes? Perhaps. With neat irony that helps us stand back and process the gore, it's the mocking eye that becomes literally the direct target of the punishment.

In remarkable contrast to all these pictures of proud and relentless grasping is Agur himself—who, remember, asked God not to make him wealthy and "full" (v 9). He warned about *adding* to God's words—wanting more. Agur in his own humility actually has eyes to see the opposite of that humility. His eyes are not lofty. They penetratingly discern the evil around him. This is a good thing: this ability to see folly and to understand where it fits in relation to wisdom (see 24:32).

More Lists—Wonderful and Awful

Agur also has eyes for wonderful things. Perhaps he is able to notice them because he is standing back and wondering at them, rather than grasping or destroying them in some way. His attitude reflects the same humble awe that his questions in 30:4 reflected, and the same admission of his need for understanding that we saw in verse 2. His attitude shapes his observations:

"Three things are too wonderful for me;
    four I do not understand:
  the way of an eagle in the sky,
      the way of a serpent on a rock,
  the way of a ship on the high seas,
      and the way of a man with a virgin." (**v 18-20**)

What common thread solves the mystery of these four "ways"? Do all these graceful movements come and go without leaving a trace, as some suggest? Perhaps. All these movements occur in the place given to them—where they fit—and they show progress and beauty within those bounds. The eagle is made for the sky; a serpent's body is made to slither along a rocky surface; a ship is made to cut through the water; and a man and woman are made for each other.

Waltke suggests that the numerical sayings in general aim for the preserving of social order through the renouncing of pride and greed (*The Book of Proverbs Chapters 15 – 31*, page 482). Indeed the self-exaltation—the reaching for more and more—does break down order (as in the order of family relationships). And **verses 18-20** celebrate order—with everything beautiful in its place. It seems fitting that the final wonderful "thing" should be the coming together of a man and a woman in the sexual union of marriage; the goodness of this climactic item in the list stands out especially in contrast to the evil of what comes next.

After the four wonderful "ways" comes one more "way," in **verse 20**. It's "the way of an adulteress," and it is out of order. Her sinful union with a man is to her nothing more than a casual meal after which she wipes her mouth and says, "I have done no wrong." She's taken her fill, outside the bounds of marriage—and with her negative example comes a turning back to a more negative list: that of four over-reachers.

The earth cannot bear up under the four things found in **verses 21-23**—four instances of people in one way or another wrongly changing status—and so the earth itself trembles and moves from its proper place. These verses seem to describe the rewarding of people who are not wise, and who are all categorized along with **verse 22**'s fool. They will always want more. As an example of a maidservant displacing her mistress (**v 23b**), Hagar, the Egyptian servant of Sarah, **Abraham**'s wife, might be mentioned. When Hagar had conceived when Sarah couldn't, Hagar "looked with contempt on her mistress" (Genesis 16:4). It's the self-exalting heart inside a person that is the issue.

It is important to remember that the history of Israel is a history of the lowly being raised: of slaves being freed and becoming a great nation; of a prostitute named Rahab and a poor widow named Ruth joining the family line of a king; of fishermen leading a church built on the foundation of a carpenter's son from Nazareth. The recurring pattern of God's working is that humility comes before honor. How does this happen? We need to learn from the ants.

Final Lists and a Final Warning

The last two lists are delightful. Notice that most of the human beings are removed from the scene; in fact, it might feel like a kind of reproach to us that the only section of creatures called "wise" is about ants, rock badgers, locusts, and lizards (Proverbs **30:24-28**).

But of course that's the point. These are "small" things, "but they are exceedingly wise" (**v 24**). What is the nature of their wisdom? Each is limited: the ants are "not strong" (**v 25a**); the rock badgers are "not mighty" (**v 26a**); "the locusts have no king" (**v 27a**); the lizard is so small it fits in your hand (**v 28a**). Along with that list of negatives, however, comes a list of corresponding and remarkable positives: the ants gather all their needful food while they can (**v 25b**); the rock badgers make the rocky cliffs into a refuge (**v 26b**); the locusts "march in rank" even without a leader (**v 27b**); the tiny lizard finds its way into kings' palaces (**v 28b**).

These "wise" small creatures are living with the grain of the created order, not against the grain. They are like the eagle and the snake, living productively according to what is given them—living, we might say, in submission to their Creator. These little creatures' lots seem especially limited, but their rewards are especially notable. Through his observations about the natural world Agur is speaking into human experience; he is recommending the lowly way, the way of humility—which is the way of wisdom, grounded in the fear of the Lord.

As we have noted already, this is the way our Lord Jesus showed fully to us when he made himself nothing, taking the form of a servant, being born in the likeness of men—humbling himself by becoming obedient to the point of death, even death on a cross (Philippians 2:7-8). Such a change in status surely made the earth tremble. But he rose from the grave, having accomplished the work of our salvation, and ascended into heaven—our risen and eternal King. Jesus, our wisdom from God, shows us wisdom's way of humility, which leads to honor. Agur, like Paul (Philippians 2:5), is saying that we should let this mind be in us.

The final list offers four things that are "stately" in their "tread" or "stride" (Proverbs **30:29-31**); they walk with confidence. In contrast to the lowly creatures we've just seen, these creatures seem to have been given a kind of innate "highness"—well, all except the final one. The lion ("mightiest among beasts"), the strutting rooster, and even the he-goat are all doing what they are made to do; the king, by contrast, joins this list as "stately" only when his army is with him (**v 31b**).

No judgment is made, and so we are left guessing how exactly to take this king. It's possible he's the highest on the list: the shining human exemplar of the stateliness glimpsed among the beasts (like the man and the woman in **v 19**). He ought to be. We yearn for such a king. But it seems quite possible that there is at least an implied warning here for imperfect kings (and perhaps for kings and nobles in training), who might be tempted to strut like roosters but who, left alone, might turn tail and run.

Such a warning is made explicit in **verses 32-33**:

"If you have been foolish, exalting yourself,
   or if you have been devising evil,
   put your hand on your mouth."

There it is, just as in Job (Job 40:4): a call to humility. In the context of the whole chapter (and book), it's a call to fear the Lord, listening to his word and walking humbly in his ways. Agur would say the Lord's "way" is too wonderful for him; he does not understand it. And yet, in his humility, he has begun to understand it, and he has communicated it to us in ways that penetrate our imaginations and our hearts.

The final three pictures of Proverbs **30:33** do not let us conclude sentimentally. Milk curds, a bloody nose, and strife are the results of all kinds of "pressing"—and so we are warned, with the most down-to-earth pictures, of the results of self-exaltation.

Questions for reflection

1. Agur has a way with pictures! Which one (or two!) stays in your mind, and why?

2. How does the culture around us encourage us not to be humble and lowly?

3. How does this call not to exalt ourselves relate to the call to follow the Lord Jesus?

13. WISDOM LIVED

The final chapter of Proverbs contains first another oracle, and then the famous epilogue to the book: the poem about the "excellent wife." After addressing this brief oracle, we'll give the bulk of our attention to the book's epilogue, letting it help us conclude this discussion of the book of Proverbs. Proverbs will send us out the same way it called us in, telling us to seek wisdom, beginning with the fear of the Lord.

King Lemuel

Proverbs **31:1-9** delivers another oracle of another man unknown to us (see 30:1)—except that he is a king. This is King Lemuel speaking, but we're told he's quoting words his mother taught him. How lovely to see, here at the end, a son who listened and learned. And how encouraging, after seeing the mother *not* blessed (30:11) and the mother *scorned* (30:17), to find a mother honored by her son.

The oracle gives a negative command and a related positive command. The negative command: kings must not give themselves to women and alcohol, lest they forget their duty to defend the rights of the afflicted (**31:2-5**). The positive command: defend the rights of the afflicted (**v 6-9**).

The son doesn't leave out the personal part of the oracle, given passionately by his mother. Maybe she saw him already failing in these ways; what parent cannot identify with her cry, "What are you doing, my son?" (**v 2**). We hear her plea: *Do not give up your energy and focus to sinful excesses* (in this case, with women and wine) *that will disable you* (see 23:29-35) *from fulfilling a true king's* *calling.* Powerful rulers encountered these temptations in a powerful way; King Solomon himself desperately needed this wisdom (see 1 Kings 11:1-2).

The negative command is crucial, but it must not obscure the related positive one. Our tendency might be to focus more on the debilitating effects of alcohol and women than on the king's calling. Yet the thrust of this oracle is the specific calling of a king to defend the afflicted; this is the duty that King Lemuel's mother warned him would be neglected through such excesses. This is the point. Lemuel's mother has taught her son the calling of a king: to defend the poor and needy (Proverbs **31:9**), who here include the "afflicted" (**v 5**), "the one who is perishing," "those in bitter distress" (**v 6**), those in poverty and misery (**v 7**), and the mute and the destitute (**v 8**). From his position of power, he is to lift up these needy ones, *opening his mouth* to speak for them, and to "judge righteously" on their behalf (**v 8-9**).

As we read this overwhelming list of kingly tasks to be performed on behalf of the most needy, what king comes to mind? When **John the Baptist** sent his messengers to Jesus to ask him if he was truly the promised Messiah, Jesus answered:

> "Go and tell John what you have seen and heard: the blind receive their sight, the lame walk, lepers are cleansed, and the deaf hear, the dead are raised up, the poor have good news preached to them." (Luke 7:22)

King Lemuel's mother did not know she was describing the promised King to come in the line of David. The prophets described him with increasing clarity. Isaiah, for example, made clear the coming King's lineage, his wisdom (note the fear of the Lord right in the center), his righteous judgment on behalf of the poor and meek, and the power of his word:

> "There shall come forth a shoot from the stump of **Jesse**,
>   and a branch from his roots shall bear fruit.
> And the Spirit of the LORD shall rest upon him,

the Spirit of wisdom and understanding,

the Spirit of counsel and might,

the Spirit of knowledge and the fear of the LORD.

And his delight shall be in the fear of the LORD.

He shall not judge by what his eyes see,

or decide disputes by what his ears hear,

but with righteousness he shall judge the poor,

and decide with equity for the meek of the earth;

and he shall strike the earth with the rod of his mouth,

and with the breath of his lips he shall kill the wicked."

(Isaiah 11:1-4)

King Lemuel's oracle is the last mention of kings in Proverbs. It is a glimpse of the king's true calling, from the lips of an unknown king. It's a passage that leaves us leaning forward to find the true king, even in the midst of sinful ones who need to learn to control their appetites for women and wine.

The Poetic Finale

We've heard Proverbs' wise writers talking about kings, but we've heard them talking even more about women. It seems utterly appropriate that Proverbs should end with a woman, after all the female figures we've met in the previous 30 chapters. Scholars debate whether this final portrait is part of the words of King Lemuel. Perhaps the chapter develops logically, with an initial warning not to chase after many women followed by a command to find just this one excellent woman and marry her! The poem of Proverbs **31:10-31**, however, holds together as a literary unit, as we will see. Whether or not it comes from Lemuel, it clearly provides an endpiece for the entire book. With amazing artistry, this poem of the "excellent wife" brings together all the book's themes in one culminating poem-portrait of wisdom at work.

These verses form an acrostic poem: the twenty-two verses begin consecutively with the twenty-two letters of the Hebrew alphabet.

It's what we in English might call "The A to Z of Wisdom." Several psalms use this poetic form, most famously Psalm 119, which gives eight verses to each Hebrew letter. The format suggests a comprehensive treatment of a subject: in Psalm 119, of the word of the Lord. The Proverbs 31 poem gives a comprehensive treatment of wisdom in action, in the life of a wife.

This poem is Proverbs' finale in a number of ways, not least in its poetic intricacy and excellence. What a shame it would be to rip it from its context as the final poetic piece in this whole magnificent wisdom book. Proverbs points us to wisdom with the most artfully shaped words, both in the more flowing passages of Proverbs 1 – 9 and also in the nuggets of condensed proverbs for which those earlier chapters prepare us. Chapter 31's poem is like the **octaves** and **arpeggios** that bring a symphony to its conclusion: the themes resound for a final time, with exuberant decoration, giving a fitting end to the whole work of art.

Who Is This Woman?

Before we draw conclusions, we need to take time with the poem. Let's make three initial observations about its subject. First, as most agree, *the Proverbs 31 woman is a real-life woman.* Proverbs has developed two categories of female figures. In chapters 1 – 9, female *personifications* of wisdom and folly picture the two ways that lead either to life or to death. Throughout the book, *real-life women appear*—from adulteresses (sometimes called "forbidden women") to mothers, to wise wives and foolish wives, and so forth. The wife of Proverbs 31 is solidly planted in a particular home and family and profession; we have no convincing reason to regard her as a picture of wisdom rather than as a real woman living it out.

The second observation, in the context of the book, is that *this woman is Proverbs' portrait of the wife a man should seek.* Proverbs' perspective has consistently been that of a son receiving words of wisdom from a father or a wise speaker—including wisdom concerning which women to follow and which to avoid. The prologue lets us understand that we can all learn from this wisdom; we readers have shared the son's perspective, for all of us must learn to turn away from folly and follow the path of wisdom. Following the perspective of the book, then, Proverbs 31 is not written to women to instruct them in how to be good wives; it is written to men (and to all of us) to instruct them (and all of us) in what we should seek. Without a doubt, wives can and should learn from this poem. But wives are not the primary audience. We'll come back to this.

Third, *the Proverbs 31 woman is meant to show us wisdom in action*. This poem brings to a climax Proverbs' teaching on wisdom. When we read **verses 10-11**, for example, we hear echoes of chapter 3:13-15. The resonances are strong: the goal in both passages is to "find" (**31:10**; 3:13) this wife/wisdom, which is "more precious than jewels" (**31:10**; 3:15). The "gain from her" in 3:14 is echoed in **31:11**, where the husband "will have no lack of gain" (these are different Hebrew words for "gain," but similar concepts).

> May we never take this Proverbs 31 poem out of its context. In order to understand this portrait, we have to lead up to it with the entire book.

May we never take this poem out of the context of the wisdom book which it brings to conclusion. We are meant to make these obvious connections with what has come before (and we'll see more). This poem offers a climactic live portrait of the same wisdom we have come to know from the start. In order to understand this portrait, we have to lead up to it with the entire book, starting with the fear of the Lord as it is presented, gradually illumined, and then finally wrapped up in this poem.

Getting the Shape

An acrostic poem by its very nature tends to jump from one idea to another, rather than having a clear logical development. Acrostic poems are like puzzles with many pieces—sort of like the book of Proverbs itself. But this poem does have discernible sections. The introduction (**v 10-12**) sets forth this excellent wife; the main body of the poem (**v 13-27**) shows her in action; the conclusion (**v 28-31**) steps back and lets us hear praise resounding in her honor.

Structural markers help: the word "excellent" appears in **verse 10** and then in **verse 29**, bookending the poem. The husband in particular plays a key part in the poem's structure, appearing at the beginning (**v 11-12**), in the middle (**v 23**), and at the end (**v 28-29**). The wife is given to us in relation to her husband; that is the context where the wife fits, and where she thrives.

Proverbs has shown us things that are "fitting" and "not fitting." In chapter 30 we observed with Agur the ways of eagles and serpents and ships—and men and women—all beautiful when they "fit" well in the places given them, showing grace and progress within those bounds (30:18-20). We saw the small wise things that accomplish amazing feats, ending up even in palaces. This wife exemplifies those ways and those things, accomplishing amazing feats as she lives out wisdom as a wife. And so, from their various places, all those around this woman harmoniously celebrate her excellence.

Organizing the main body of the poem becomes more challenging. These verses are reminiscent of the prologue's kaleidoscopic nature, in that there is no neat division: the categories of "home" and "outside the home," for example, keep overlapping. Family and community relationships keep mixing—just as they do in the book, and in the course of real life.

The wife's foundational relationship with the Lord is mentioned only at the poem's end (**31:30**). This climactic mention of the fear of the Lord provides a bookend not for this poem but rather for the book as a whole. The fear of the Lord was introduced as wisdom's foundation

(1:7); it bookended Proverbs' first section (9:10); it served as a strong thread binding together the proverbs (for example, in 15:33 – 16:9); and now the fear of the Lord pulls together the entire book (**31:30**). For all its swirls of verses, Proverbs is a literary work with a remarkably coherent shape. The fear of the Lord holds it together.

This is a strong poem celebrating a strong woman, and the very shape of the poem reflects her strength. The acrostic format sets forth solid building blocks that create a comprehensive and sturdy structure. The poem's main sections encase this woman securely in the relationships of her life, all in their proper places even as they expand before our eyes.

Having glimpsed the context and the poetry that bring this woman to us, we are now ready to get to know her better.

An *Eshet Hayil*

The Hebrew words for the woman introduced in **verse 10a** (*eshet hayil*) have been translated "excellent wife" (ESV), "wife of noble character" (NIV), "virtuous woman" (KJV), "valiant wife" (Waltke, *The Book of Proverbs Chapters 15 – 31*, page 510), and "noble woman" (Longman, *Proverbs*, page 535). "Valiant" and "noble" get at the tone of this phrase and this poem, which (as we've said) is strong. There are even military overtones; for example, Longman translates **verse 11**'s "gain" as "plunder," as the word technically refers to the spoils of warfare (page 542-543). This woman literally "**girds her loins** with strength," and her arms are strong (**v 17**).

This description of wisdom lived out with valiant strength fits the glimpses we've seen throughout the book. Proverbs never presents wisdom as some abstract, ethereal quality or as some academic subject, unrelated to the hard knocks of life. No, from the start wisdom shows up in the streets and the marketplace, unafraid to call out fools in public, crying out for people to listen. Wisdom is pictured not as sitting quietly but as building a house, hewing pillars, slaughtering beasts, and mixing wine (9:1-2). Wisdom was the "master workman" at creation (8:30)! Wisdom is strong in the most concrete way.

In some Hebrew Old Testament manuscripts, the book of Ruth follows the book of Proverbs. Proverbs 31's poem, then, would lead directly into a named, historical example of an *eshet hayil*. At a crucial point in the narrative of Ruth, she is blessed by Boaz, who tells Ruth that everyone in town knows she is an "eshet hayil" (Ruth 3:11). The widow Ruth has faithfully cared for her mother-in-law Naomi, leaving behind her own land of Moab to return with Naomi to Bethlehem, and declaring allegiance to the Lord God of Israel (Ruth 1:16). In Bethlehem, Ruth has worked humbly and hard in Boaz's fields, gleaning barley from morning till night (Ruth 2). This is one strong *eshet hayil*!

Ruth is an important *eshet hayil* to note, for, even while resonating with the truths of Proverbs 31's *eshet hayil*, her strengths unfold quite differently. Ruth is a poor widow with no children, not a well-to-do wife with husband and children like the woman of Proverbs 31. This is crucial to remember as we take this poem to heart, aiming to live out wisdom's strength in the various concrete contexts of our lives.

Questions for reflection

1. In what ways does the oracle from King Lemuel speak to you today?

2. How do you find it helpful to view Proverbs 31's poem as the conclusion to the whole book?

3. A "strong woman" can mean a lot of different things! How would you characterize the strength of this excellent woman?

PART TWO

What Kind of Work?

Five specific observations about the woman of Proverbs 31 will enable us to understand this portrait of wisdom in ways that speak not only to those who are married or contemplating marriage, but also to all of us human beings as we hear wisdom's call.

The first three observations relate to this woman's work. First, *she works hard*. She's the opposite of the sluggard. The book's theme of hard work and its rewards (versus laziness and its rewards) comes to completion in this woman. This is a portrait in action, with verse after verse of busy productivity: making fine garments and textiles (Proverbs **31:13, 19, 22, 24**); procuring and preparing food for her household (**v 14, 15**); buying property and planting vineyards (**v 16**); selling garments (**v 24**); instructing others (**v 26**). **Verse 27** sums it up:

"She looks well to the ways of her household
   and does not eat the bread of idleness."

That seems like an understatement! And on top of all that, she gets up before dawn to prepare the meals (**v 15**) and "her lamp does not go out at night" (**v 18b**), perhaps meaning she stays up late to work (or that she's provided plenty of oil to keep the lamp burning).

Second, *the Proverbs 31 woman works willingly to serve those around her.* **Verse 13b** is lovely: she "works with willing hands." Do you know people like this, who make you feel like they are privileged to serve you? I'm sure Ruth did that for Naomi. I have sons and daughters-in-law who make me feel that way; they *want* to clean up after a meal, it seems—they do it with willing hands.

The woman of Proverbs 31 is not working simply for her own advancement and her own good. Her "household" is mentioned four times (**v 15, v 21**—twice—and **v 27**), and closest to her in the household is her husband. The enclosing structure of this poem—with the husband at beginning, middle, and end—shows that all this woman's work is done in the context of this marital relationship and with a central goal of doing him "good, and not harm" unceasingly, "all the days of her life" (**v 12**). This wife is embracing her wifeship. If you are married, then your spouse is your closest and most important human relationship; you have become one with that person, even as God declared from creation (Genesis 2:24). In earlier chapters we discussed the centrality of marriage in wisdom's instruction, the evil of adultery that breaks the marriage covenant, and the teaching of Scripture that unfolds to reveal marriage as a picture of Christ and his church.

When the excellent wife embraces her wifeship, she embraces this good plan of our Creator, and she goes to work within its bounds—as a wife. We will see that her work reaches far, but even in its farthest reach it is not unrelated to her relationship with her husband. He's right there in the center of her poem, sitting among the elders of the land (Proverbs 31:23). She is lifting him up with all her work, which is praised not just by her husband but also "in the gates" (**v 31**).

Third, *this woman makes things in her work.* She's not plodding away doing the same things over and over again thoughtlessly. Her mind is working as well: she doesn't just buy a field, but she "considers" a field and buys it (**v 16**). And she makes money from the sale; that "fruit" perhaps allows her to plant the vineyard. In **verse 18**, she "perceives that her merchandise is profitable." That means she evaluates her gifts and understands that they are worth something—not just financially, but indeed financially. This woman is, through her work, creating new things: imaging the Creator God who made the world and made us in his image to be little creators after him as we steward his creation.

We have noted the theme of making clothing and textiles. **Verse 19** gives a live picture of her hands at work in each line, holding the **distaff** and then the **spindle** as she spins the thread to weave her fabrics. The picture is of a woman interacting creatively with God's creation. **Verse 14** may suggest a curiosity to explore creation, comparing her to "the ships of the merchant" as "she brings her food from afar." Maybe her own business takes her to explore new markets, where she finds some interesting foods to bring home; maybe she enjoys creating some new menu items now and then!

We human beings are made to work hard and make things. The stuff of making doesn't have to be textiles or foods—perhaps it's words, or some form of technology or science, or flowers or crops, or painting, or music—the possibilities are endless. The Proverbs 31 woman is wonderfully challenging in the same way that the whole book is challenging, as it invades all the nooks and crannies of our lives to demonstrate wisdom's transforming work. Those many glimpses of the sluggard should tell us that we sinful people will be tempted to stay in one place without doing much or taking risks or over-exerting ourselves. Proverbs would tell us that hard work—willing, servant-like, creative work—will bring glory to our Creator and great good to all those around us.

But this portrait of all this work is exhausting—and unrealistic, we might say! In one sense it is. We are not likely to run into the Proverbs 31 woman who is presently doing all the things listed in this poem. I've attended several funerals lately for faithful Christian women, and for each one, as I've read the obituary, I've thought, "Wow! I had no idea this woman did all these things!" The summaries of lifetimes of faithful work are truly impressive—whereas I only knew these women at certain stages or only in certain moments. The summaries don't include all the times of leisure or rest or sickness or incapacity or failure. They list mainly the various involvements and relationships and accomplishments. The obituaries of these women were not extraordinary; these were not famous or wealthy women. They were women whose lives were full of labor for the Lord, in all kinds of ways, as indeed our lives should be. They spurred me on, even as the Proverbs 31 woman is meant to spur us all on; this is the kind of lived-out wisdom we should seek.

Reaching Beyond

The fourth observation about the Proverbs 31 woman is that *she cares for the needy.* She is generous. Right after watching her hands working that spindle, we see her hands again:

"She opens her hand to the poor
and reaches out her hands to the needy." (**v 20**)

We've observed the increasingly strong themes of justice and generosity toward the needy throughout Proverbs. Earlier in this chapter we heard that final call to the king to "defend the rights of the poor and needy" (**v 9**). Here is this woman doing that—not just opening her hand to give but reaching out her hands, plural (**v 20**), perhaps to give more, or perhaps to lift up or embrace a needy one.

This woman provides regularly not just for her immediate family but for others, including her "maidens": that is, her maidservants. Hers is clearly a well-to-do household, but not a stingy or ingrown one. She has understood the truth that to oppress a poor man is to insult his Maker, but "he who is generous to the needy honors him" (14:31; see also 19:17).

> This woman is not just opening up her hand to give but reaching out her hands to embrace.

Proverbs 14:31 and 19:17 are important reminders that underlying and prompting all this action is a certain kind of heart. Beyond all this woman's human relationships is a relationship with her Maker: that is, with the Lord God. Here's the fifth and final observation: *the woman of Proverbs 31 fears the Lord.*

The first sign of her relationship with the Lord comes in 31:26, which addresses her tongue. After the many, many proverbs we've read about the tongue, here is just one verse addressing it in this climactic poem—perhaps illustrating the restraint of speech that all those proverbs advised. This woman is characterized more by her actions than by a lot of words (see 20:6).

When this woman does speak, however, wisdom comes out, and "the teaching of kindness is on her tongue" (**31:26**). That word "teaching" comes from the Hebrew *torah*, or "law," and the word "kindness" from the Hebrew *hesed*, often translated "steadfast love," as in the Lord's unfailing love for his people. On this woman's tongue is the word and the love of God himself. She has obviously taken in that word: "the wise of heart will receive commandments" (10:8a). That word flows from her heart, in her words, making her wise teaching like "a fountain of life" to those around her (13:14).

How did all this wisdom grow in this woman? She fears the Lord (**31:30**). Other possible fears are mentioned in this poem: **verse 21**, for example, tells us, "She is not afraid of snow for her household, / for all her household are clothed in scarlet." She does not entertain even the most common fears for the safety and well-being of her loved ones, for she has made them clothes of scarlet—meaning either clothes of fine fabric or clothes of double thickness which are extra warm.

Is all this clothing literal, or is it symbolic? We might be tempted to answer "symbolic" when we read in **verse 25** that "strength and dignity are her clothing"—this verse clearly turns these noble qualities into metaphorical clothing that both adorns and protects her. So is the family's fine warm clothing part of the picture as well, perhaps symbolizing the security of wisdom's protection? Are the woman's fine linen and purple garments there to picture her regal dignity and strength? Yes, and no! The poet is describing real clothing in the lines that are not directly metaphorical. However, the effect of all this fine clothing is more than literal; it creates an impression of richness and security that suggests the spiritual richness and security of wisdom—a richness and security that can be found in the poorest and simplest households where only the Lord is feared.

The joyful security found only in the Lord is most wonderfully communicated as this woman "laughs at the time to come." This woman lives in relationship with the Lord, fearing him and following his word, and so she has confidence in the future, knowing her hope will never be "cut off" (23:18). It's not that she thinks bad things won't happen; she knows "the righteous falls seven times and rises again" (24:16). She is walking the path of the righteous, that keeps getting brighter until full day (4:18). Her eye is on treasure that lasts. She found the beginning of wisdom and is following it to the end:

"Charm is deceitful, and beauty is vain
> but a woman who fears the LORD is to be praised." (**31:30-31**)

Conclusion: Praise!

The poem of Proverbs 31 concludes with *praise* (**v 28, 30, 31**)—not just indirectly from this woman's children but directly from her husband, who speaks the words that echo the poem's first line, telling her she is the most excellent of all (**v 29**)! How fitting that others, and not the woman herself, put forward her accomplishments, especially after Agur's (and the book's) emphasis on wisdom's humility.

The poem broadens in the end, from the praise of the woman's immediate family, to the praise of her works in the city gates (**v 31**). That's where we first met Wisdom crying out: in the streets, in the markets, at the head of the noisy streets, and "at the entrance of the city gates" (1:20-21). We've come full circle, but we end not with wisdom's personification calling out but with the real life of a woman of wisdom calling forth praise. *Seek and celebrate this eshet hayil to live with as your wife,* Proverbs says to young men. *And seek this life of wisdom,* Proverbs says to all of us.

When I teach on Proverbs 31, someone almost always asks whether this portrait of a wife might point ahead to believers as the bride of Christ. My first response is always to caution against making that kind of quick leap, rather than taking the text, in its immediate context, to speak of a wife and a life of wisdom in the way we have understood it. But of course we cannot end the book of Proverbs without acknowledging again, as we have throughout, that the fullness of wisdom has been ultimately revealed to us in Christ our Savior, for he is our wisdom from God (1 Corinthians 1:24).

Every time we New Testament believers say "the fear of the Lord," we speak those words with their meaning more fully understood than in Old Testament times, for we have seen the fulfillment of all Yahweh's promises to his people in the Lord Jesus Christ. When we see Proverbs' emphasis on relationships—first and foremost our relationship with the Lord—we should stop to praise God for fully accomplishing the salvation that makes that relationship possible, through his Son. When we read in Proverbs about the righteous king, we should find our thoughts turning to King Jesus who came to show that righteousness, and to give that righteousness to us, by bearing our sin in our place, on the cross.

The life of wisdom shown to us in Proverbs is finally and fully a life lived in Christ—with his word and his Spirit lighting up all the concrete experiences of our everyday lives. The pastor Ray Ortlund writes that "wisdom is the grace of Christ beautifying our daily lives" (*Proverbs: Wisdom that Works,* page 17).

It is true that we do not live in Christ merely as individuals but as his body, the church—his bride (Ephesians 5:22-33; Revelation 19:6-9). Even though the writers of Proverbs did not know the full story of redemption, they pictured a wife as the final portrait of wisdom lived out. Resonances—beautiful resonances—do emerge when we read Proverbs 31 with the full light of the gospel shining back on it, showing us this bride in action. There is indeed much grace in the truth that we believers live out this high calling not individually but all together, uniting our gifts and our wholehearted work all for the glory of the One who laid down his life to redeem us. These are the things I say, carefully, after that first caution not to jump there too quickly.

May this wisdom book help light our path of following Christ together as his people. May Christ himself light up the meaning of these God-breathed words of wisdom. May our hearts be full of praise to the Lord for "the depth of the riches and wisdom and knowledge of God" (Romans 11:33), all made known to us in Christ. May we look forward with confidence to the fullest praise around the heavenly throne of the Lamb:

"Amen! Blessing and glory and wisdom and thanksgiving and
honor and power and might be to our God forever and ever!
Amen!" (Revelation 7:12)

Questions for reflection

1. What aspects of this excellent woman's work do you find most challenging, and why?

2. Do you laugh at the time to come? What does that mean? (See also Psalm 112:7.)

3. How would you sum up in your own words the way this book points you to the gospel of Jesus Christ?

GLOSSARY

Abraham: the ancestor of the nation of Israel and the man God made a **covenant** with. God promised to make his family into a great nation, give them a land, and bring blessing to all nations through one of his descendants (see Genesis 12:1-3).

Allegorical: expressing a hidden meaning using symbolic figures, objects, or stories.

Aloe: a type of succulent plant or the juice derived from it.

Anointed: chosen or appointed. (In Old Testament Israel, kings were anointed with oil to demonstrate that they were the king or the heir).

Antithetic: contrasting or opposite.

Apostle: a man appointed directly by the risen Christ to teach about him with authority.

Arpeggio: the notes in a musical chord played one after the other.

Atone: to make a way of coming back into relationship with someone by dealing with the problem that has existed between the two parties.

Beatitude: an explanation of how to live in a way that brings the joy of acting in line with God's will in his world.

Bride of Christ: the church (that is, all Christians) is described in this way in 2 Corinthians 11:2; Revelation 19:7-8; 21:9.

Chaff: the unwanted part of a head of grain.

Commentator: the author of a commentary, a book that explains parts of the Bible verse by verse.

Common grace: good things which God gives regardless of whether someone is a Christian or not (e.g. rain, oxygen).

Convert: someone who has changed religion.

Covenant: a binding agreement between two parties. God made a covenant with **Abraham** in Genesis 12 – 17, and with his people, Israel, at Mount Sinai (Exodus 19:1-8).

David: the greatest of Old Testament Israel's kings.

Day of wrath: the day when God will bring judgment, promised throughout the Bible. Also called the Day of the Lord.

Discrete: separate, distinct.

Distaff: a stick or staff around which coarse wool is wound ready to be spun.

Elder: men in Old Testament times who were the leaders of Israel (or, in some contexts, of their tribe or their family). In the New Testament and in our own times, elders are men who are responsible for the teaching and ministry of a local church.

Ephah: a unit of measurement, used for dry goods. Equivalent to around 6 gallons or 23 liters.

Epilogue: concluding section in a book or play.

Epistle: a letter.

Fall: the moment when Eve and Adam disobeyed God and ate from the tree of the knowledge of good and evil (see Genesis 3).

Fallen: affected by God's judgment, which was a consequence of the fall.

Fear of the Lord: respect and reverence for God.

Garden of Eden: the flawless place God gave the first humans in which to live, enjoy his presence, and work for him (Genesis 2:8-17); also the scene of those humans deciding to rebel against God's rule, part of the judgment for which was being shut out of Eden (3:1-13, 23-24).

Gird your loins: literally, to tie up a long tunic around the waist and groin, to prevent it getting in the way of running or fighting. This image means preparing yourself for a difficult task.

Glean: to gather the last bits of grain from the edges of a field after the farmer has harvested the majority.

God-breathed: 2 Timothy 3:16 says that the Bible was "God-breathed" or "breathed out by God." This means it comes directly from God.

Godhead: God, existing in three Persons, which are each distinct from one another and are each fully God, of the same "essence" or "Godness." We usually call these three Persons Father, Son, and Holy Spirit.

Herod: Herod Antipas, the first-century Jewish ruler of Galilee and Perea under the Romans, who played a role in the executions of both John the Baptist and Jesus.

Hin: a unit of measurement, used for liquids. Equivalent to around 1.5 gallons or 6 liters.

Immanent: existing in the world and able to be experienced.

Iniquity: sin or wrongdoing.

Inspired: in this context, meaning coming directly from God. The word literally means "breathed into."

Interpretive grid: the framework each of us has in our minds, based on our own experiences, opinions, and values, which helps us to make sense of the world.

Ire: anger.

Jesse: the father of King David.

Job: the main character of the book of Job: he is a righteous man who is tested by Satan.

John the Baptist: Jesus' relative, and a prophet whose role was to announce that God's chosen King (Christ) would shortly be arriving in Israel, and to call people to turn back to God as their Ruler in preparation for Christ's arrival. See Mark 1:4-8.

Lake of fire: a picture in Revelation which represents God's judgment on sinners (see Revelation 19:20; 20:10; 20:14-15; 21:8).

Last Supper: the meal which Jesus shared with his disciples on the night he was arrested (see, for instance, Matthew 26:17-30).

Legalistic: the belief that the way to please God and/or have a place in heaven is to obey a set of rules sufficiently well.

Lot: casting lots was a way of making a decision by chance, similar to rolling dice.

Meditation: focusing and reflecting on something, especially a Bible passage, over a period of time. This biblical sense is different from Eastern religious meditation, which often involves trying to empty the mind rather than to fill it.

Meter: in this context, meaning the rhythm of a line of poetry.

Moralistic: the belief that what matters most in life is how someone behaves.

Moses: the leader of God's people at the time when God brought them out of slavery in Egypt. God communicated his law (including the Ten Commandments) through Moses, and under his leadership guided them toward the land he had promised to give them.

Myrrh: a perfume derived from tree resin.

Noun: a person, place, or thing. In many languages, nouns are thought of as having a gender. For example, in Spanish a village is masculine, while a city is feminine.

Objective: based on facts, not feelings or opinions.

Octave: two sounds which are eight notes apart: the highest and lowest notes on an eight-note scale; or the whole run of eight notes.

Parallelism: the use of two lines or sentences in poetry that link to each other in some way.

Pentateuch: the first five books of the Bible.

Pentecost: a Jewish feast celebrating God giving his people his law on Mount Sinai (Exodus 19 – 31). On the day of this feast, fifty days after Jesus' resurrection, the Holy Spirit came to the first Christians (Acts 2), which is why Christians tend to use the word "Pentecost" to refer to this event.

Personification: when an object or idea is represented as a person.

Pontius Pilate: the Roman governor of Judea at the time of Jesus.

Redeem: to free, release, or buy back.

Redeemer: in this context, someone who restores a close relative's rights or avenges his or her wrongs (see Leviticus 25:25-55; Numbers 35:18-21). Specifically, a redeemer might buy a relative back from slavery, buy back the property of a relative who had had to sell it due to poverty; avenge murder, marry his brother's widow in order to have a child who would be an heir for his brother, or receive an agreed payment to make up for wrongdoing to his relative. In the book of Ruth, Boaz is a redeemer for Ruth and Naomi; he buys Naomi's field and marries Ruth, the widow of his relative.

Redemptive work: the process throughout history by which God has and will rescue his people from sin to live in relationship with him forever.

Refrain: repeated phrase or lines in a poem or song.

Rhetoric: the art of persuasive public speaking.

Sage: in this context, a wise person.

Saints: Christians. The word literally means "holy ones" or "distinctive ones."

Saul: here, referring to the first king of Israel.

Sanctify: make holy or make more like Christ, by the work of the Holy Spirit.

Seed: here, meaning descendant or offspring.

Sermon on the Mount: the term used to describe a sermon Jesus gave to a huge crowd on a mountainside, which Matthew recounts in Matthew 5 – 7.

Serpent: Satan is represented by a serpent in Genesis 3.

Sheol: Hebrew word for the underworld, where the souls of the dead go.

Sluggard: a lazy person.

Sovereign: having supreme authority and complete control.

Spindle: a stick which wool is wound around as it is spun (twisted) into yarn.

Synonymous: two words meaning the same thing.

Synthetic: bringing two ideas together.

Theological: theology is the study of what is true about God.

Transcendent: beyond our comprehension; existing beyond the physical world.

Transgression: sin or wrongdoing.

Trials: difficulties in life, which may test us and our faith.

Word: Jesus is called the Word of God in John 1. This refers to the fact that God spoke the world into being (so Jesus as the "Word" is the one God spoke through; see Genesis 1; Psalm 33:6) and that God reveals himself in Jesus (see Hebrews 1:2).

BIBLIOGRAPHY

- Graeme Goldsworthy, *Proverbs: The Tree of Life* in the Reading the Bible Today series (Aquila Press, 1993, Kindle edition)

- Ed. Wayne Grudem, *The ESV Study Bible* (Crossway, 2008)

- Derek Kidner, *Proverbs: An Introduction and Commentary* in the Tyndale Old Testament Commentary series (IVP Academic, 1964).

- Derek Kidner, *The Wisdom of Proverbs, Job and Ecclesiastes: An Introduction to Wisdom Literature* (IVP Academic, 1985)

- C.S. Lewis, *Reflections on the Psalms* (Harcourt, Brace & World, 1958)

- Tremper Longman III, *Proverbs* in the Baker Commentary on the Old Testament Wisdom and Psalms series (Baker, 2006)

- Raymond C. Ortlund Jr., *Proverbs: Wisdom That Works* in the Preaching the Word series (Crossway, 2012)

- Leland Ryken, *Words of Delight: A Literary Introduction to the Bible* (Baker, 1987)

- Bruce K. Waltke, *The Book of Proverbs Chapters 1 – 15* in The New International Commentary on the Old Testament series (Eerdmans, 2004)

- Bruce K. Waltke, *The Book of Proverbs Chapters 15 – 31* in The New International Commentary on the Old Testament series (Eerdmans, 2005)

- Lindsay Wilson, *Proverbs: An Introduction and Commentary* in the Tyndale Old Testament Commentary series (IVP Academic, 2018)

Proverbs for...
Bible-study Groups

Kathleen Nielson's **Good Book Guide** to Proverbs is the companion to this resource, helping groups of Christians to explore, discuss, and apply the wisdom of this book together. Eight studies, each including investigation, apply, getting personal, pray and explore more sections, take you through the book. Includes a concise Leader's Guide at the back.

Find out more at:
www.thegoodbook.com/goodbookguides

Daily Devotionals

Explore daily devotional helps you open up the Scriptures and will encourage and equip you in your walk with God. Available as a quarterly booklet, *Explore* is also available as an app, where you can download Kathleen's notes on Proverbs, alongside contributions from trusted Bible teachers including Tim Keller, Mark Dever, Al Mohler, Stephen Um, Sam Allberry, and Ray Ortlund.

Find out more at:
www.thegoodbook.com/explore

More For You

Exodus For You

"The book of Exodus is key to understanding Jesus. It is an exciting story, a historical story and—as it points us to and inspires us to worship Jesus—it is *our* story."

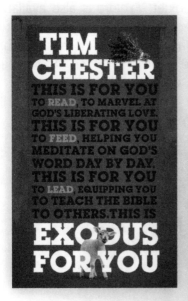
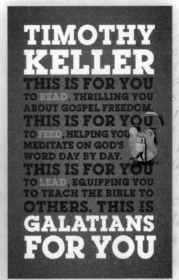

Galatians For You

"Galatians is all about the gospel—the gospel all of us need throughout all of our lives. It's dynamite, and I pray that its powerful message explodes in your heart as you read this book."

The Whole Series

- **Exodus For You**
  Tim Chester
- **Judges For You**
  Timothy Keller
- **1 Samuel For You**
  Tim Chester
- **2 Samuel For You**
  Tim Chester
- **Psalms For You**
  Christopher Ash
- **Proverbs For You**
  Kathleen Nielson
- **Isaiah For You**
  Tim Chester
- **Daniel For You**
  David Helm
- **Luke 1-12 For You**
  Mike McKinley
- **Luke 12-24 For You**
  Mike McKinley
- **John 1-12 For You**
  Josh Moody
- **John 13-21 For You**
  Josh Moody
- **Acts 1-12 For You**
  Albert Mohler
- **Acts 13-28 For You**
  Albert Mohler
- **Romans 1-7 For You**
  Timothy Keller

- **Romans 8-16 For You**
  Timothy Keller
- **1 Corinthians For You**
  Andrew Wilson
- **2 Corinthians For You**
  Gary Millar
- **Galatians For You**
  Timothy Keller
- **Ephesians For You**
  Richard Coekin
- **Philippians For You**
  Steven Lawson
- **Colossians & Philemon For You**
  Mark Meynell
- **1 & 2 Timothy For You**
  Phillip Jensen
- **Titus For You**
  Tim Chester
- **James For You**
  Sam Allberry
- **1 Peter For You**
  Juan Sanchez
- **2 Peter & Jude For You**
  Miguel Nunez
- **Revelation For You**
  Tim Chester

Find out more about these resources at:

www.thegoodbook.com/for-you

the good book
COMPANY

BIBLICAL | RELEVANT | ACCESSIBLE

At The Good Book Company, we are dedicated to helping Christians and local churches grow. We believe that God's growth process always starts with hearing clearly what he has said to us through his timeless word—the Bible.

Ever since we opened our doors in 1991, we have been striving to produce Bible-based resources that bring glory to God. We have grown to become an international provider of user-friendly resources to the Christian community, with believers of all backgrounds and denominations using our books, Bible studies, devotionals, evangelistic resources, and DVD-based courses.

We want to equip ordinary Christians to live for Christ day by day, and churches to grow in their knowledge of God, their love for one another, and the effectiveness of their outreach.

Call us for a discussion of your needs or visit one of our local websites for more information on the resources and services we provide.

Your friends at The Good Book Company

thegoodbook.com | thegoodbook.co.uk
thegoodbook.com.au | thegoodbook.co.nz
thegoodbook.co.in